THIS THING
CALLED
LOVE

ANGELA R. CAMON

Order this book online at www.trafford.com
or email orders@trafford.com

Most Trafford titles are also available at major online book retailers.

Printed in the United States of America.

ISBN: 978-1-4907-1611-4 (sc)
ISBN: 978-1-4907-1630-5 (e)

Trafford rev. 02/25/2014

www.trafford.com

North America & international
toll-free: 1 888 232 4444 (USA & Canada)
fax: 812 355 4082

Contents

Introduction

ONE OF THE MOST INFLUENTIAL people in a girl's life is her father. A father has such a big impact on the growth and development of his daughter in regards to how she matures from being a totally dependent cute and cuddly infant to being an independent toddler, transitioning into those hormonal years better known as adolescence and finally into a strong and confident woman.

A father's role is essential in his daughter's life. His role can be the determinant factor of whether she gets involved in a healthy relationship or in an unhealthy one. A daughter's first bond with any man should be between her and her father. It is through this bond that she learns how another man should treat her. This relationship is the building block for future relationships with the opposite sex. It is typical for a daughter to gravitate toward a man who treats her the way that her father did. If her father was loving, accepting of her, provided her with stability, she will gravitate toward a man who provides those same type of characteristics. However, if a father caused hurt, whether emotional, physical or mentally, a daughter may pursue a relationship with a man who constantly causes pain in her life. She will repeat what she knows rather than what she wants, even if that means being involved in an unhealthy relationship.

Fathers are essential to the process of building a daughter's self-confidence, self-esteem, self-worth and self-reliance. Some girls go through periods of uncertainty, especially during the adolescent years. It is during those times that a father's role is very significant. A father, who offers verbal words of encouragement, is alert to his daughter's needs and sensitive to her feelings, is engaged in her life, both physically and emotionally, and takes an active interest in things that she is involved in, sends a positive message to his daughter that she is important to him. This will help diminish her insecurity and increase her belief in her own abilities.

Daughters that grow up with a healthy father-and-daughter bond are often less likely to become a teenage mother, experience depression, experiment with drugs and alcohol, develop body image problems and engage in criminal activity. Whereas daughters who do have not father in their lives can experience a plethora of problems. Research says that daughters who do not have a healthy father and daughter bond are often challenged with poor self esteem, depression, anger, and fear of rejection, failed romantic relationships, the need to seek approval from others. They are more likely to engage in aggressive behavior, become single parents, and receive welfare, drop out of school, and experience mental and emotional health problems.

It is unfortunate, but there are many of daughters who have not had the privilege of growing up with their fathers in their lives. The absence of fathers in the lives of their daughters has become an epidemic that has plagued our society and affects many families from all walks of life. As a result, this has caused a detrimental impact on the entire life of his daughter including the decisions that she makes and her attitude, actions and beliefs about the various issues, which often times result in negative behaviors.

There are many fathers who are physically present, but are emotionally absent. The father is physically present in the home, supplying the basic needs of clothes, food and shelter for his daughter but he is emotionally distant to what is going on in his daughter's life. This can have just as much devastating effect on his daughter as him not being present at all. It is not enough for a father to be present in his daughter's life; he must also be actively involved in her life.

Follow the journey of a young girl who shares her story about her life and the various hardships that she experienced as a result of living with a physically present but emotionally absent father.

HOW IT ALL BEGAN

Chapter 1

M Y MOM AND DAD BOTH attended the same high school. He was a junior and she was a sophomore. At the time they didn't know one another. Until one day my dad saw my mom standing in the lunch line. Mesmerized by her long silky black hair, the enchanting spark in her eye, her flawless skin and her big dark lips, my dad was captivated by my mother's beauty. Her winning smile made her presence known whenever she entered a room. At least my dad was aware of her presence. He was drawn to her at first sight, and instantly made his own personal vow that he would pursue her until she became Mr. Michael Alexander. This was not as easy as he perhaps thought that it would be. Just as my dad was aware of my mother's presence, she too was aware of his and quite frankly, she was not impressed.

Sure there were some good things about him. He indeed had some good qualities, but there was also a grey side to him. In my mother's opinion, the bad outweighed the good. He was just not her type.

My dad was popular, especially with the girls because he was the star quarterback on the football team. He seemed to always have an entourage who answered to his every beck and call. On game day, he would choose one special girl who would have the distinct honor of being with him. Being with him supposedly meant that you were special. He would shower "the lucky girl" with money and other meaningless material things. They were meaningless because they did not come from his heart. The material things that he gave and the way that he treated the girl to make her feel special was only a precursor for what lied ahead. In a conniving way, he would somehow convince the girl that she was special to him by telling her what every girl wants to hear, and that is that she is loved. With a warped sense of reality, the girl thinks that she can seal the deal by offering her most prized possession, which is her virginity. She has sex with him, only to find out that she is not special to him and he didn't have good intent on committing to her as he had promised.

My mom was different. She stood out like a sore thumb because she was not intrigued with being his side kick. She had more respect for herself and had set high standards. She did not just associate with anybody. It took more than a guy telling her that she was pretty or fine to get her attention. He had to have something going for himself. She wasn't so shallow as to think, that a boy had to be a certain height or weight or things of that nature, but she focused on more important issues such as does he go to church, is he doing well in school, or how does he treat females? She was more interested in his character rather than how well he dressed or the material things that he could give. Based on those criteria alone, it was apparent that my dad was not my mother's type. It was clear that they both were on a different course in life. She was making decisions that would lead to a bright future, while my dad was living for the moment. The course that he was taking was leading to destruction.

Among the decisions that my mother made, the most profound was accepting Jesus as her personal Lord and Savior, at an early age. That decision was the foundation for all the other decisions that she made. One of the decisions that took a great deal of courage and faith was her decision to remain abstinent until marriage. Although most of the girls were engaged sexually, my mother once again stood out like a sore thumb because she was not involved sexually with anyone. She was so passionate about her decision to wait to have sex until she was married, that she persuaded her friend to make the same decision. She and her friend made a pact that they would wait until they got married to have sex. They were the best of friends and would often talk about life and how one day they would get married. They had already decided what kind of husband they were going to marry, what kind of house they would live in, what kind of cars they would drive and how many children they would have. For many years, they held on to their pact. From time to time, they would ask each other "are you still holding on?' What they were really asking each other was "are you still a virgin?" Usually, they would each reply, "Yeap, I'm still holding on". But one day, when they are doing "virginity check", as my mother referred to them, she found out that her friend had broken their pact. My mother's friend had had sex with her boyfriend in the backseat of his car. My mother was not only hurt because her friend broke their pact, but also because of the pain that her friend was experiencing. She had sacrificed her precious gift of her virginity only to find out that her boyfriend was not in love with her as he proclaimed. He only saw her losing her virginity as a game. Once he had sex with her, he was ready to move on to the next girl. This left my mother's friend distraught. Not only was she carrying the emotional baggage from the guilt of having sex in the first place, but now she had to deal with the shame of being manipulated by her boyfriend.

This was not the kind of life that my mother wanted to live. In order to avoid this happening to her, she knew that she had to stay clear from the path of guys like my dad.

But my dad had other intentions. He had every intention of capturing my mother's attention and romancing her to make her his own. In his own subtle way, he was determined to make my mother fall in love with him. In the beginning when he tried to make small talk with my mom, she would not give him the time of the day. But over time he began to make small changes. As he made noticeable changes, my mother began to let her guard down and started entertaining the idea of getting to know him better. It wasn't easy, but he eventually convinced my mom that he had changed. He was no longer the same. After many failed attempts to get my mother to say yes, she finally agreed to go on a date with him. That date lead to other dates and the rest is history from there. They continued to date throughout the remaining of their high school years. Shortly after graduation, my dad popped the question and asked my mom to marry to him. Of course she said "yes".

My parents had a small traditional wedding with a few family and friends there to celebrate. Life as a married couple was great.

They adored one another and that was reflected by the quality time that they spent together. It was said that that when you saw one you saw the other. They were inseparable.

Finding out a year or so later, that my mom was pregnant with my brother Charles brought even more happiness to their relationship. My mom said that my dad was like a child eagerly waiting for Christmas presents on Christmas morning. He could hardly wait for my brother to be born. When Charles had finally made his grand entrance to the world, he immediately became the apple of my dad's eye. My dad went from impatiently waiting for Charles' arrival to anxiously waiting for him to grow up. He was excited about the opportunity to do father and son things together like going fishing. Every day he would talk to Charles, as if he understood, telling him of the things that they would do together.

Life couldn't get any better in my dad's eyes. His family was growing and he and my mother were happy, he had a job to work to take care of his family. Although there were times that it seemed they were barely surviving, as far as my dad was concerned, he was content. His dream of having a son had been fulfilled and he was satisfied. He was very adamant about not having any more children. My mom on the other hand entertained the idea quite frequently in her mind of having more children one day.

They had had many discussions before about adding to the family when Charles got older. Each time my dad would outweigh my mom with the many reasons why they shouldn't have any more children. From time to time my mom would bring the subject up of having another baby in hopes that he would change his mind. But to no avail. One of the main reasons that he objected having any more children was because of the financial obligation. My dad would count up the cost about everything. He did not like to spend money at all, but especially if it was not necessary. To him, having another baby was not necessary.

Knowing the reason behind my father not wanting to have any more children, my mom decided that she would get a job to help with the family expenses. She did not have any particular job in mind; just something that she could do that would require only a few hours of her time. From past discussions, she already knew that my dad did not want her to get a job because he strongly believed that her rightful place was to be at home taking care of my brother Charles. He held to his belief that children are impressible at a young age and that is why the mother should have the greatest impact on the child.

She understood the importance of her role as a mother and she embraced it. In fact, she embraced motherhood so much that she wanted to have another baby that was the whole reason behind her wanting to get a job in the first place.

She was willing to do whatever she needed to do in order to help provide for her family. In order to get back and forth to work, she knew that she had to have transportation; so she convinced my dad to take her car shopping.

He was not convinced that getting another car was a good decision so he did not make any promises to her about buying a car, they were merely looking. At least that is what he thought. Little did he know that there was more to come.

My mom and dad went to a car lot in a city called Nashville that was about ten miles from where they lived. She was immediately drawn to a shiny red Mercedes Benz 500R r that was situated on the highest car rack twirling on display for the entire world to see. It was advertisement at its best.

With child like excitement, my mom raced to the car of her dreams if nothing more than to touch it. My father tried to calm her down, but it was too late she was already emotionally invested.

My dad searched around to see the practical cars that were in their price range, while my mother stood mesmerized over the car which my dad decided that they could not afford. In the back of her mind she knew that they could not afford it, but it did not hurt to dream. Depending on the job that she got, this dream might be able to be a reality.

As she continued to scope out the other cars, a tall, bright skinned man with, lean shoulders and tight abs walked up to her. He called her name "Rebecca? Rebecca Alexander? Is that you?" as if he knew her in times past. To my mother's surprise it was one of her old boyfriends.

His name was Frank Simmons. He and my mother had dated for a couple of years in high school and when they graduated they went their separate ways. They had lost track of one another. Apparently Mr. Simmons had moved back into the area and bought several businesses. One of which happened to be the car lot, hence the name Franks Auto Sales. He and my mother talked trying to catch up from what had been happening in each other's lives.

They continued to talk and talk, eventually the talking led to laughing and the laughing led to a friendly hug. My dad did not see it that way though. He saw a man talking, laughing and now hugging his wife. It was the friendly hug that caused a spark of jealous to rise up in my dad. He asked Mr. Frank "are you trying to sell my wife a car or something else. He made it very clear that he did not like the attention that he was giving my mother. He might have really freaked out if he had known that this was one of my mother's old boyfriends. It was apparent that my dad was jealous of the way that Mr. Frank was embracing my mom especially when he insisted that they go to another car lot. He was very determined that they were not going to buy a car from this car lot. Even if he had to drive 10 or 20 extra miles to get to the next car lot, he would do it. My mom insisted that Mr. Frank had not done anything to cross the line.

My father might have made his point about not buying a car at Franks Auto Sales, but he was unaware that there was a possibility that this could be my mother's place of employment. During their conversation, my mom had mentioned to Mr. Frank that she was looking for a job. Knowing the potential that my mom has and the belief that she would be an asset to his company, Mr. Frank had offered her a position on his staff.

With mixed emotions, my mother accepted the job that Mr. Frank was offering. He offered her a leadership position which sometimes required her to work closely with Mr. Frank. My dad was not in agreement with my mom working at all, but especially not with Mr. Frank. What made matters worse was that there were occasions that she had to work at night.

My mom had been working at Franks Auto Sales for about 6 months when she found out that she was pregnant with me. Although she had prayed to God to one day have another child, this pregnancy happened at a time that she was not anticipating. She had planned to work for a while, save some money and then have another baby. That was her plan, but apparently not God's. She thought about the scripture in Isaiah 55th chapter that says "For my thoughts are not your thoughts, neither are your ways my ways," declares the Lord. "As the heavens are higher than the earth, so are my ways higher than your ways and my thoughts than your thoughts". This pregnancy had indeed caught her by surprise, but nevertheless she was still excited about having another child. It might not have been planned by her and my dad, but she always said that no pregnancy is a mistake, even if the parents don't plan it. She believes that God has a plan and purpose for everybody's life and she was certain that God had a plan for my life. She knew that my dad would not share the same sentiment. She knew that he would not be able to fathom in his mind that this is a blessing from God. She couldn't help but wonder if he didn't consider this as a blessing, how his reaction would be? What would go through his mind? I guess that is the reason that she waited as long as she could before she even tried to tell my dad that she was pregnant. When she finally did get up enough nerve to try to talk to him, he would ignore her. He would not give her the time of day. He seemed to always be too preoccupied with something else. The cycle continued with her trying to share the news with him and him not paying attention.

A couple of weeks had passed by, and my dad still did not know that my mom was pregnant. She made several attempts to try to tell my dad that she was pregnant with me, but for some reason she couldn't keep his attention long enough to tell him the news. As time went on, she began to experience symptoms of being pregnant. She was already having morning sickness. When my dad asked her why she was vomiting so much, she brushed him off by saying that she probably had a virus, knowing full well that she was pregnant.

It wasn't long before my dad found out on his own. The way that my dad found out that my mom was pregnant with me is perhaps the cause of the tension between me and my dad. I wished a thousand times that my mom had found a way to tell my dad, instead of letting him find out the way that he did. One day my dad was taking out the trash and as he was emptying the trash, he saw one of the many pregnancy tests that my mom had used. My mom had taken several pregnancy tests; I guess she was trying to convince herself that it was indeed true that she was pregnant.

With rage in his eyes, and trembling in his voice, he held up the pregnancy test and asked my mom about it, "What is this"? She immediately went into defense mode, and tried to recount the times that she had tried to talk to him. My dad was beyond angry with my mom because he felt that she had betrayed him. At one point he even accused my mom of being pregnant by Mr. Frank Simmons. I don't know if he really believed that or if he was just saying that to hurt my mom. But regardless she was appalled by this accusation. She took her marriage vows serious and would never do anything to violate them.

From this point on their relationship was never the same. This brought tension between them that intensified each day. Their communication had broken down so, that they were barely on speaking terms. It was that way for the entire pregnancy. My mom did all she could to try to convince my dad that this was an act of God and things would work out alright. She really believed that God had a purpose for my life. But he insisted that if she had not prayed about having another baby then maybe she wouldn't be pregnant. Either way he felt that it was my mom's fault that she was pregnant and he couldn't find it in his heart to forgive her. My mom went from being his sweetheart to the traitor, or as he referred to her as his evil betrayer.

THE DAY I WAS BORN

Chapter 2

THE DAY WAS FINALLY HERE. It was February 7, 1994, the day that I Stacey Alexander was to be born. For most, it was one of the happiest days in Alexander family, but of course it was not for my dad. This is the day that he had dreaded for the past nine months. From the time that my dad had found out that my mom was pregnant with me, up until now, he made it very clear that he was not excited about having anymore children. While he was overjoyed when he found out that my mom was pregnant with Charles, he was disappointed to find out about my conception. He was very content with it being him, my mom and my brother Charles as a family.

He was not happy about having a new baby and his actions proved it. He did not go to any of my mom's doctor's appointments like he did when she was pregnant with my brother. He didn't do any of the exciting things that he did like rubbing my mom's stomach to make the baby move and kick, and singing and talking to the baby inside, and listening to the baby's heartbeat like he did the first time she was pregnant. From time to time, he would glance at my mom's stomach, but only when she would hold up her shirt to show him how fast the baby was growing. The more my mom tried to get him involved with the pregnancy, the less interested he seemed and the more disengaged he became.

Surprisingly, he did muscle up enough concern to at least drive my mom to the hospital when she went into labor, but that was the extent of it. Instead of being in the labor room with my mom, he

9

chose to sit in the waiting room. He filled his time with tedious tasks like filling out a crossword puzzle and watching the 6:00 news instead of taking the opportunity to witness the monumental occasion of the miracle of life being brought into the world.

The time had finally come. I was born at 12:36 pm. I weighed 7lbs 19 in. My dad sat in the waiting room unaware of the event that had just transpired. Although he lacked the enthusiasm of my birth, there were many others who rejoiced and gave thanks to God for the new addition to our family. My grandmother Mattie, my aunts, uncles, cousins all gathered around waiting with anticipation for the time that I would be taken to the nursery. They could hardly wait to cast their eyes on me.

Finally, coerced by one of the nurses to join the rest of the family, he walked down the hall to the nursery. Nurse Judy and my dad had a conversation:

NURSE JUDY
(stroking the baby's hair)

What a beautiful baby! She has a head full of hair. Isn't she beautiful?

MICHAEL
I guess so!
NURSE JUDY
She looks just like you. I know you are proud.
MICHAEL
(speaking in a harsh tone)
She doesn't look a thing like me. Not all.
NURSE JUDY
Did you see her beautiful hair?
MICHAEL
And? What's so special about hair?
NURSE JUDY
(apologetic)

Oh I didn't mean to offend you. I just thought that her hair was beautiful (sneering) I'll have to admit I just had to touch. It feels just like silk.

MICHAEL
(shouting)
There isn't anything special about her. Not her hair, not the
way that she looks. There is nothing special about her.

NURSE JUDY
Oh Mr. Alexander, I beg to differ. She is special indeed.
MICHAEL
You are raving on about how beautiful her hair is, but did you see
her short stocky arms and leg? Why are her eyes slanted? What about
that spot on her face? Did you see that?
NURSE JUDY
Mr. Alexander, you will have to look past what you see on the
outside and find out what is on the inside. I've seen hundreds of
babies born at this hospital and all of them are special.

MICHAEL
The way she looks, I can't take her around. She
will be the most embarrassing thing to me.
NURSE JUDY
There is something extra special about this baby.
She is going to do great things. You'll see!
MICHAEL
Yeah you think so? Well I don't.

A week later my mom and I came home from the hospital. She
was so glad to be home. She gave me a tour of every room in the
house just like she did when she brought my brother home for the
first time.

Since my dad had never held me before, my mom asked him if
he wanted to hold me. She felt that if he held that he would connect
with me and we would bond together. He said no at first, but because
of her persistence he finally grabbed me out of her arms and held me
for a few brief minutes. He looked at my mom and said "Now! There
I held her! Now are you satisfied"? That was the longest that my dad
held me for the first months of my life. He made it very clear to my
mom that he was not going to take an active role in my life. In a loud

stern voice, he told my mom "Listen you are not going to force this baby on me. Don't be expecting me to hold her and feed her, walking off he shouted and I don't do diapers". Devastated about what my father had said, my mom pleaded with him trying to convince him to see the significance of both of them taking an active role as a parent, and emphasizing that I needed both of them. Regardless of what my mom said, and how much she tried to win him over, he did not give in. He gave her the clear indication that she was in this thing all alone. My dad acted as though my mom had cheated on him with another man and I was the product of an affair. But that was not the case at all. Deep down my dad knew that my mom had not had an affair, he was just too proud to admit that God had worked a miracle.

He told her "I'll take care of "your daughter" because it is the law but I don't have to love her. Can't anybody make me love her either. My mom said "Michael nobody should have to make you love your own daughter. It should be automatic". He in turn replied well, I don't love her. I didn't ask for her. She is just another responsibility for me. I don't need her in my life.

With tears streaming down her face, she said "You are going to regret the day that you ever said that".

The day that my father vowed that he would never love me or accept me as his daughter, resonated in my mother's spirit for years. More than likely, my father probably didn't give it a second thought about what he had said. But little did he know that those very words that he said on that day would later come back to haunt him.

GROWING UP

Chapter 3

G ROWING UP AS A CHILD, I watched as my father work long, hard, and tiring hours on his job trying to provide for his family. He always made sure that we had food on the table so that I didn't have to go to bed hungry. I always had nice clothes to wear. They were not always name brands and in fact some were hand me downs from the thrift store, but they were nice and clean. He provided a nice 4 bedroom 2 bath home for us to live in.

My father believed in working hard and preserving during hard times. He instilled those values in both me and my brother. I had all that I needed as far as material things were concerned, but I still was missing one very important thing in my life. I desperately needed my father's love and affection. I longed to hear him say the most three important words that every little girl needs to hear her daddy say, "I love you" and to feel his fatherly affection and approval.

As a young child, I was willing to do anything that I could to have my dad's undivided attention. I remember vividly one morning; my dad was getting ready to go to work. I went into his room and asked him to take me to the park. I would see the other children's fathers pushing them in the swings or catching them as they came down the sliding board. I wanted to experience the feeling of having my father catch me or push as I swing as highest I could go. I asked my dad to stay home with me and he told me that he had to work. With a young child's inquisitiveness I asked why he had to go to work. He in turn explained that it was because he had to make money to take care of the family. I asked him how much money did he make on his job? At first he was hesitant, but eventually he told me that he made $10.00 an hour. I ran to my bedroom and got my piggy bank. I pour out my money and began to count it. It was ten dollars exactly. I handed it to my father and told him that I would pay him so he wouldn't have to go to work and he could spend time with me. It was at that moment that I realized that my life would be a struggle. My father felt that his only obligation to me was to provide for me financially. But what he did not realize was that I needed so much more. He did indeed provide the essential material things that I needed in life for survival, but emotionally and spiritually I was bankrupt. He never took the time to deposit seeds of encouragement and words of approval that I needed to hear. What he poured into my spirit was the message that I was not loved or wanted by him.

It was difficult to understand why it was so hard for my father to love me. I wondered what made me so unlovable. Why wasn't I his pride and joy? Why didn't he ever smile at me? Was it because I am a girl and different from my brother? Was it because I was overweight? Did he think that I wasn't smart enough? Why couldn't he get past the way that he found out about me? Did he really believe another man was my father?

I would often pray to God about my relationship with my father. I wanted things to be different between us. I wanted to see a change in him.

I used to hear Mr. Thomas, an elderly man who lived in our neighborhood talking about the difference between being a father and a dad. He said a father is a person who provides a seed to father a child, but a dad is someone who takes the time to get to know his child. A dad is concerned about the things that are going in his child's life. He enjoys spending quality time with his child, but most importantly he shows unconditionally love. Anybody can be a father, but it takes a real man to be a dad. I knew him as my father, but I wanted to know him as my dad. Out of respect, I called him dad, but it didn't mean anything. It was just a title that he had. It was certainly not based on the relationship that we had.

I continued to pray for my father. Although it seemed that the more I prayed for him the worse things got. I was praying for my dad to make a change and he did. But unfortunately it was a change for the worse. As time went on, my dad developed a drinking problem. He said that he had to start drinking in order to cope with me. It started with him having a few beers occasionally at home on the weekend, but that quickly escalated when he started going to the bar throughout the week. His drinking was affecting every aspect of his life. It affected his performance on his job. It affected how he treated me and my mother. We never knew what kind of mood that he would be in when he came home. I can remember one time my dad came home late from work. It was around 11pm when I was curled up in my bed, snuggled tightly under the warm covers, that I was startled by his loud thunderous voice. My heart was palpating. My skin was clammy. Fear wrenched my nerves to the point that I was shaking because my dad had to pass by my bedroom to get to his. I thought for a moment, maybe this time he would go straight to his room without stopping by mine. But no such luck. With a half empty bottle of beer in his hand, he stumbled into my room and started shaking my bed, pulling the covers off of me, yelling at me "Get up! Get up! You are always whining about spending time with you. Well I'm here now! Let's spend some time together now. I work hard trying to provide for you and you don't even act like you appreciate it. You don't do anything to help out around here. You can't even keep your room clean".

As he was throwing my clothes around in my room, he looked on my dresser and saw my progress report from school. I had 2 D's, one in Math and another in reading. He gave me his usual speech about how stupid I was and how I would never be anything. He pointed out how my brother Charles was always doing well in school, but I was the one who was always falling behind. I tried to convince my dad that although in my mind I thought that I was doing my best, I would try to do better. I would do whatever I had to do to make him proud. My dad was quick to tell me that he would never be proud of me and that my best would never be good enough for him. He ended his escapade with a door slam so loud that it could pierce an eardrum.

He left my bedroom and made his way to his bedroom and in a child like manner; he took my progress report to my mom. He was waving it in the air as if he had the evidence that he needed to prove his case that I was stupid. He showed it to my mom, as if she had not seen it. She told him that she knew about my grades and was confident that with a little more support and encouragement I would bring my grades up. That was not what my dad wanted to hear. I could hear my dad say to my mom" I don't know why you invest so much time in her anyway. It makes more sense to push Charles ahead. He is the one who makes all A's. Now he is the one who is going to be somebody one day. He is going to be the one who takes care of me when I get old too".

My mom usually didn't talk to my dad when he was not sober because she thought that it was pointless. But this time she did. She told him "they are both my children and I love them the same. They both need encouragement, and I'll give it to the both of them as long as I live. She looked deep in his eyes and said "Don't be surprised that the child who you think is never going to be anything or ever amount to anything just might be the child who you need one day. Mark my words!!

I lay in my bed thinking about what I had heard my mom say. What did she mean when she told my dad, "Don't you be surprised that the very child that you ridicule just might be the one that you need one day? Did she know something that we didn't? Had God told her something, or had he shown her a vision?

Hours passed by and the break of morning had set. It was morning and as with each morning I got up with the expectation that today would be different. Maybe today would be the day that my dad would realize how much precious time we are missing with not spending time together. Maybe today would be the day that I will be able to look in my dad's eye and see the love and instead of looking down as I pass by him. Maybe, just maybe today will be the day that my dad will say that he loves me.

I gave it a test to see if maybe this could be the day. I walked to his room to speak to him. I merely said "Good morning". His response was "what's so good about it". It was as if the very sight of me turned his stomach. He began to argue and complain about things that I had done or at least he thought that I had done from weeks and in some cases months ago. My dad was not in the mood to be nice or friendly to anyone but especially me. Maybe one day, but this was definitely not the day.

I went back to my bedroom, pacing back and forth across my floor, with tears rolling down my face, I said a prayer to God. "Dear God, I don't know what I did for my daddy not love me. But please Lord, let me feel my daddy's love one day". I got dressed and did what I normally did on Saturdays. I cleaned the house from top to bottom. I went to the storage closet to get the supplies that I needed to do my daily chores. I got a broom and mop and some floor cleaner that smelled like citrus fruit and some lemony fresh furniture polish to dust the furniture in the living room. My mom was very adamant about having a clean house and one thing that she would not tolerate was having dust all over her good furniture. She took pride in how our house looked. She didn't believe in cutting corners not when it came to getting things for the house. She had all kinds of products to keep our house smelling fresh and clean. She had invested in so many vacuum cleaners that she could probably start her own cleaning company. Every new model that came out she would just have to try to see if it worked better than the one she already had.

I took all of my supplies and headed to the hallway leading to the living room. I took my time to sweep every corner of the floor. After sweeping the floor, I mopped the floor and gave it a shine so bright that you could easily see your reflection. I was proud of the work that I had done. It was so clean that it was fit for a king to eat off of. Or so I thought. But my dad seemed to think differently. He came and grabbed the mop out of my hand and starting hitting me with it. He threw me against the wall and then he looked at me in my face and said 'that's what happens when you do things wrong. I had a big blue and black bruise on my right arm from being hit with the mop and a knot was on my head when he pushed me against the wall.

All I could hear in my mind was yelling "you can't ever do anything right. According to my dad, I never did anything right. I always messed things up. He said that I would never be anything. Based on his physiology I would never be successful because I struggled in school. I will not be able to make a living for myself because I couldn't even manage to sweep and mop a floor. My dad thought that I would always have to depend on somebody to take care of me, and he made it very apparent that it was not going to be him. He longed for the day when he didn't have to take care of me anymore, and would be able to have something for himself. I was always the blame for him not being able to keep money in his pocket.

But things were different when it came to my brother. My brother could ask for anything that he wanted, and my dad would somehow make a way for him to get it. It was a known fact, at least in my opinion that my dad worshipped the ground that my brother walked on. In my dad's eyesight, my brother could do no wrong. He definitely approved of brother much more than he did me. He had such high hopes for my brother's future. He was certain that my brother would be successful at whatever he decided to do in his life. It didn't matter what career that he chose, he was going to be on top. The way I saw it, there wasn't much difference between me and my brother. Sure we had our own way of doing things, but we both had dreams of doing something great. The only difference was that my brother had the support of my dad to encourage him and to believe in him; while I on the other hand struggled to shine in his eyes. I longed to hear him say "I'm proud of you" or "Keep up the good work" but I never heard those words come from my dad. The familiar tune of hearing my dad ask me "why can't you be like your brother", made me sick to my stomach. I thought if he asks me that one more time I am going to scream. Each time that he would ask me I thought the same thing, that I would scream, but I didn't instead I just listened to him taunt me with his rude comments and his expressions of disappointment of me.

When my father wasn't ridiculing me, my mom became his target. I was accustomed to hearing my dad yell at my mom telling her that she was an unfit mother because I was 14 years old and still didn't know how to clean a house. I would hear him tell her that I would never get married because no man wanted to marry a fat slob. That is how my father referred to me because I was overweight. He told her that she would always have to take care of me because I would never make anything out of myself. But I remember very distinctly what my mom said one day when my father was carrying on with his usual cynical remarks about me. In my defense, my mother said "Be careful what you say because that child that you talk about and think will be nothing, might be the very child that have to take care of you one day. Mark my words. Watch what I say". I had heard her say this before, but I still did not understand what she meant. I just know that what she said stuck in my mind.

My dad was full speed into his arguing that my mom's comment didn't seem to faze him in the least bit. He continued on his rampage about how I could never do anything right. My mom had said what she had to say to my dad, and then she was quiet. I figured she was doing what she always did when my dad wanted to argue, and that was to pray. I used to wonder why my mom didn't argue back with my dad. Could it be that she was afraid of him? When I asked her she would always quote this scripture, "A soft answer turned away wrath, but grievous words stir up anger". She said that it only made matters worse if she argued back, so she would just be quiet and let my dad cool down.

I wished my dad would remember that scripture when it came arguing at my mom and me. Every day my dad made it a point to let my mom know exactly how much she frustrated him. Not a single day went by without him trying to start a fight with my mom. Sometimes it was a small bicker but at other times it was a full-blown heated argument. It seemed that my mom always said something or did something that set my dad off. It wasn't necessarily that it was my mom's fault because to be honest, it really didn't take much to get my dad upset.

Sometimes it could be something as simple as having too many lights at one time or leaving a light on when you leave a room, or me not sweeping the floor good enough for him, or they would argue about bills. Although I am just a child, but in my opinion, this is where all of their arguments stemmed from; not having enough money to pay the bills. I always thought that my dad was frustrated about not having money to pay the bills so he would take it out on us. Sometimes I would get the mail out of the mailbox, and hide the bills from my dad. I have a feeling that my mom knew what I was up to, but she never said anything. I guess she was like me; in desperate need for peace and would do just about anything to get it.

LOOKING FROM THE OUTSIDE IN

Chapter 4

From the outside looking in, everything appeared normal. It appeared as though we were the typical family. My dad went to work every day to provide for the family. He had a friendly disposition at least with everyone else. I would see my dad smile when he would talk with his friends, but when he got home he was fussing and yelling at me like being home was the last place he wanted to be. By the way he act, it seemed that he was one of the easiest guys to get along with. He put on such a front about how blessed he was to have us in his life. Actually he was blessed to have us, but he didn't truly know how blessed he was. My mom cooked a three course meal every day and would have it hot and ready when he got home. There were times that she would cook and my dad wouldn't eat just because he thought that it didn't look good. I used to wonder how my mom could continue to put up with my dad and his ways.

Everything seemed normal from the outside world. All of my friends envied my life for a number of reasons. For one thing I had both my mom and dad living with me. When I would complain about my dad throwing his fits as I called them, they would always say, "Girl at least you have your dad living with you". Most of my friend's dads were not living with them. I even had a friend who had never met her dad. My family was blessed to live in a big 4 bedroom 2bathroom house with a white picket fence. They all lived in public housing or what some call "the projects". These houses were run down and not well maintained. The neighborhoods were infested with drug dealers and drug users and gang bangers. It was common to see paramedics and police officers bombarding the neighborhood because there was always so kind of trouble going on especially on the weekends. Compared to their lives, I guess was in better shape, but I knew that there was something missing that they could not see. They had something that I did not have. This thing called love.

I believed that my mother loved me, but then a part of me had some doubts because if she did love me, why would she continue to let my dad treat me like he did. Why didn't she leave him? Why did she stay with him and tolerate his behavior? What kind of example was she setting for me to follow? That is okay for a husband and a father to treat his family the way my dad treats us. Furthermore why did she take up for him? She would always say that my dad acted the way that he did because he was under stress. He drank because he was under stress. But what about the stress that he caused in our lives? What about the void that he left in my life?

It was a direct result of my dad's verbal abuse that caused me to struggle with a low self esteem and have to fight a battle of insecurity. Hearing my father say to my mother "I'm so embarrassed of her, I hate to take her anywhere with me" was my breaking point. In times past, I was able to push what he said in the back of my mind, but this time it got to me. I withdrew like a turtle in a shell and lost all confidence in myself. I could only imagine if my own dad was disappointed and ashamed how other people must have felt about me. I began to feel as though maybe I didn't deserve to be loved. I lived my life with the impression that something was wrong with me always in the fore front of my mind. I struggled with the complex of not liking myself and others not liking me.

MY ESCAPE

Chapter 5

B EWILDERED BY MY DAD'S CONSTANT ridicule, I quickly learned that I must fight to keep my own sanity. To escape from the pain, I faded into my own world. I escaped to a place in my mind where there was tranquility and unconditional love. I got to that place through my writing. Writing was one of my favorite things to do. When I was in my world of writing, my spirit was alive and I had a new vision about myself. I could envision myself being successful. In many ways I was successful because writing was one thing that I could do well. Writing allowed me to transcend my wildest dream. I dreamed of writing my own book and seeing it on the shelves in libraries and bookstores all across the nation. Instead of me reading somebody else's book, other people would be reading my book. That was my dream.

Other people used drugs and alcohol to escape the pain in their lives, but I chose a different route. I used writing as my therapy to get through the pain and loneliness that I had in my heart. I wrote about the good things; things that made me laugh like the fun times that I had at my Grandma Mattie's house. I loved to write about the times that I spent with my cousins Mikki and Nikki at my grandmother's house. They were twins who both were short and chubby and loved to eat. My aunt used to say, if it isn't nailed down, they will eat it. One of our favorite games that my cousins and I and the rest of the neighborhood kids used to play was tag. My cousins were easy targets because they couldn't run very fast. It was always so much fun and

I really enjoyed writing in my journal about the good times that we shared.

I also wrote about the bad things like when my best friend moved away or about the boys who I had a crush on, but would never give me the time of day. Sometimes I would just write about common things that happened at school, but every day I wrote about how sad I was because my dad did not love me. Not a single day went by that I did not write something about my father. I wrote about the things that I did not understand about my dad and our relationship. I wrote what he said about me and how he made me feel. In an effort to express the feelings that I had, I wrote a poem that I entitled "A Child's Plea".

"A Child's Plea"

A tear here

A tear there

A tear seems to be everywhere

I try so hard.

So hard I try

But you get mad and make me cry

I don't understand why you treat me the way that you do

Don't you know that I am human and I have feelings too?

You tell me to do as you say and not as you do

But I need an example set before me that is tried and true

Money, new toys and fancy clothes are nice gifts too

But the greatest gift is a simple smile and a great big I love you

What's the matter with me?

Do you wish I'd die so you could be free?

Can I trust you to tell me what is right?

I want to follow you with all my might

Do you love me, I often wonder in my mind?

You treat me as if I have you in a bind

Listen to the message that is coming from me

Give me love and encouragement that is a child's plea.

My friend Tina convinced me that I should enter my poem in the annual poetry writing contest that was hosted by our school. I entered the contest and won second place and received a silver medal. I was so proud of myself. I knew that my mom would be too, but I only prayed that my dad would be. I could hardly wait to get home to show my parents the medal and the certificate that I had received. When I got home I ran to the kitchen where I knew my mom would be. I showed her my certificate and silver medal. She grabbed me and gave me the biggest hug. I knew that she was proud but it really showed when she got on the phone and started calling what seemed to be everyone that she knew and told them about my accomplishment. She took my certificate, put it in a frame and set on the mantle for the entire world to see. She made such a big deal about me winning second place, I can only imagine what she would do if I had won first place.

My dad came home and I told him about the writing contest and the poem that I had written. He did not ask to read my poem; he did not even take the time to look at my medal or my certificate. He did not seem interested at all, so I voluntarily told him that I had won second place. Of course second place was not good enough for him. Instead of saying "Congratulations" or I am proud of you" he simply asked "Why didn't you win first place"? Oh, let me tell you why you didn't win first place. It is because your writing is atrocious; that's why". I stood there with my head held down and my heart full of regret that I had even mentioned it to him. I told my dad mom said that I did a good job; she was proud of me.

"That's the difference between me and your mom, she insists on filling your head with lies. I will tell you just like it is. I know that you have this silly dream of publishing a book, but you are just fooling yourself if you think you will ever be good enough to write a book. There is no company going to waste their time and money to publish your book. Besides I told you it takes special people to write books, and you don't qualify", my dad said to me.

I would have settled for a cold shouldered good job or some other comment, anything but why didn't I win first place? Instead of celebrating with me, he found a way to point out that I didn't quite make the mark and that I was always lacking in some area. That is how my dad made me feel.

SCHOOL DAYS

Chapter 6

TIME HAS QUICKLY PASSED BY and now our middle school years are but a distant memory. It is hard to believe that I am in high school. This was both exciting and fearful. It was exciting because of all the things that came along with being in high school, but like everyone else, I was stressing over the possibilities of having Mrs. Campbell as my English teacher. We had all heard about Mrs. Campbell while I was in middle school. Mrs. Campbell must have been in her late 50's or early 60's. She was short in statue and very petite but her size was certainly not to be mistaken for a sign of weakness. I don't believe that Mrs. Campbell had a weak bone in her body. She spoke in a loud deep monotone with a baritone pitch that would sure put the fear in anyone. She was known to chew you up and spit you out for just about any and everything. Even for simple things like not having a pen for class. She was big on her students being prepared for her class. If she caught you sleeping in her class, she would make you stand for the entire class period. Mrs. Campbell's students could expect to take a test every day. She said that the only way that she would know if her students truly understood the lesson was to give them a test. But the greatest fear that I had about being in her class, was wondering if she would like me. Most teachers accept whatever student comes in their class and tries to reach all of them regardless of whatever level they were on. From the things that I heard from the older kids in my neighborhood say, things were different with Mrs. Campbell. She had a tendency to favor those students who easily caught on to what she was teaching. She did not like to repeat a lesson that she had already taught. This is one of the things that made her furious among other things. For those students who had a difficult time learning, she did not spend much time trying to teach them, but she would push them to the side as if they did not matter. On very rare occasions she would muster up a smile for her struggling students but for those who were on top of things they seemed to be her pride and joy.

It was the first day of school my friends and I looked for our names on the roster taped to the window in front of the school. We each found our names and looked for our schedules. I found my name and then my schedule. It read: First period—Mr. Black, 2nd period—Mrs. Troutman, Third period—Mrs. Fillmore, Fourth period—Mrs. Carry, Fifth period—Mr. Drew and Sixth period—Mrs. Campbell. "My eyes fixated on the big bold black letters of her name for a brief second, but then without even thinking that Mrs. Campbell might hear me, I yelled "Oh no, I got Mrs. Campbell, Why Lord, why me"? From that very moment fear and dread set in. I was so stressed that it felt like butterflies were in my stomach.

It seemed that the day went by so fast because it didn't take long before it was time for me to go to Mrs. Campbell's class. I walked in her class carefully glance over the room to see the design of the room and to see where Mrs. Campbell's desk was located. I decided to sit in the third seat in the fourth row. I was trying to get as far away from her desk as I could. As I sat down trying to get my nerves under control, I heard Mrs. Campbell say "Take any seat you want, but don't get comfortable because I just might move you". Just then my heart seemed to sink to the floor. Now I was really afraid; what if she decided to move me closer to her. My stomach hurt so bad I thought to myself, maybe I should call my mom and tell her that I was sick and needed to go home. But then I thought what would I do for the next 179 days that I had left in school?

Mrs. Campbell began to call the roll in a synchronized remote fashion. She would call the names and the students would answer "present or here." She called "Sarah", Sarah replied "here" she called Michael's name and he answered "present". Then she came to my name. She called my name once. She called it again but before I could respond to her she called it again. But this time she said it with emphasis and she called my last name. She said "Stacey Alexander. Hmmmmmmmmm". Now why does that name ring a bell to me? She called it again, and then she asked is Charles Alexander your brother? I nodded to say yes. She said "Oh really! I enjoyed having him in my class; he was such a smart young man. I hope that you are as smart as your brother. The feeling that I felt when my dad asked me why couldn't be like my brother came surfacing to the top of my mind. For the remainder of the class, Mrs. Campbell talked about the rules of her class and her expectations of us. One of the assignments is that we will have to do book reports and do an oral presentation. I was not looking forward to that at all. I didn't mind reading the material and writing a report, but I did not want to stand before the class and talk. That was just not for me especially since one of her pet peeves is for a student to talk to low. I guess she thought that everybody should talk loud and project their voices just like she did.

In the beginning I tried to convince myself that everything would be okay and that I would make it through Mrs. Campbell class. But after two weeks had passed by and things were not any better I wasn't so sure. It was still a challenge for me to go to Mrs. Campbell class every day. What if she called on me and I didn't know the answer? What if Mrs. Campbell thought that I didn't talk loud enough?

Although I knew that there would be some challenging times in school, there were still some good things to look forward too. One of the events that every girl looked forward to was the annual Father/Daughter dance. I can remember being at school and getting a flyer at school about the annual Father/Daughter dance to take home. Although my father had never participated in an event like this with me ever before, for some reason this time I had a glimmer of hope. Maybe this would be the time that he would recognize the importance of bonding between a father and daughter. I was so excited about the possibility of going out with my father. I came home and told my mom about it hoping that she would find it in her heart to try to convince my father to go. But she jokingly told me that she was not my father and that I needed to talk to him for myself.

So I did. With fear and trembling, I went in the family room where he was watching the evening news on television. I handed him the flyer. He looked it, balled it up and threw it on the floor.

Although the cost of the dance was reasonably priced, I felt that my father was probably thinking that is an additional expense that he had not budget for rather than seeing it as an opportunity for us to create a memory. Sure enough his response was that he couldn't afford it. So I told him that I was willing to wear one of my old Sunday dresses and I would let Mrs. Mary to do my hair. Mrs. Mary was a self taught cosmetologist who from time to time did all the kid's hair that lived in my neighborhood. I kept pleading with him because I really wanted to go. I told him that I wanted to dress up and be beautiful just like the other girls. He leaned forward in his seat and said "Beautiful? Did you say beautiful? You actually think that you could ever be beautiful? You think if Mrs. Mary puts a few curls in your hair that that will make you beautiful. He laughed and said "Honey, Mrs. Mary can't work miracles. And that is what it will take to make you beautiful".

Needless to say my spirit was crushed. I was disappointed and hurt to the core. But as with past disappointments, I disguised my pain and pretended that it didn't matter. When my friend Michelle called me to see what color my father and I were going to wear to the Father/ Daughter dance, I told her that I was not going because I thought that it was silly and I had better things to do with my time. But that could not have been further from the truth. I wanted more than anything to go to the Father/ Daughter dance.

The next day all the girls in my class were talking about going to the dance. I sat my desk looking and wishing that I could partake in the conversations that were going on. But I did not have anything to contribute because I was not going. Stephanie, Jennifer and Regina did not engage in the conversations with the other girls, they sat in the back of the classroom and had their own conversation going on. I was not surprised though because that is how they always did. They would always branch off from the rest of the class, as if they were too good to be with anyone else. Most people in my class thought that they were popular, but to me they were just arrogant. Sure they wore the latest fashion when it came to clothes and jewelry and yes their parents could afford to buy them anything that they wanted, but to me that still did not make them any better than the rest of us. Most of the other girls looked up to them, and would do anything to be a part of their inner circle. But I chose not to, I would rather be who I am than to fake just to be a part of something where I did not belong.

In her high pitched proper voice, Jennifer said to Regina and Stephanie, "Father and I are going to go to the Unique Boutique on Madison Avenue to select our attire for the dance".

Regina followed by saying "I am quite sure that my mother will have something specially ordered for this most festive occasion".

Sure not to be left out of the conversation, Stephanie reminded them about the elegant dress which her grandmother purchased for $1000.00 for her to wear to last year's father and daughter dance. Stephanie said" I must say that my dress was a showstopper. I am not sure that my mother will be able to find something as beautiful as that dress around here, but it sure will be fun trying. They all three laughed.

I was sitting in a desk a row away from them and I could hear everything that they were saying. They knew that I was in hearing distance of what they were saying, which is why I believe that they talked louder just so I could hear.

In a sarcastic tone, Jennifer asked me where I was going to buy my dress for the father and daughter dance. Before I could even decide if I was going to indeed respond to her question, and if so in what manner, Stephanie blurted out, "I heard that there was a Good will Store on Park Avenue". Regina said "Isn't one of the requirements to actually have a father to come to the dance with. We all know that most of her kind don't have their fathers in their lives. They are either locked up in prison or strung out on drugs".

I was boiling hot mad, but Mrs. Campbell not knowing it, saved them from me. I gave each of them a look that signified that this matter is not over. As far as I was concerned, they were going to pay for the comments that they made.

Mrs. Campbell quiet the class down to make an announcement about the dance. She was the coordinator for the dance this year and she wanted every girl to come so that there would be a good turnout this year. She also wanted every girl to bring a picture of her and her dad. This was something that I could not do because I did not have a picture of me and my dad. She said bring a picture of one of your most favorite moments that you shared with your dad. The more Mrs. Campbell said about the pictures, the worst that I felt.

Finally, Mrs. Campbell asked every girl to raise their hands if they were planning to attend the dance and also would be able to bring a picture by that Friday. Every girl in the class raised their hand, except me. I was the only girl in the class who did not have a father who was willing to bring her to the dance and the only girl who did not have a picture of her and her father. Again I felt bad. But not as bad when Mrs. Campbell singled me out and asked why didn't I raise my hand. In my mind it should have been clear why I didn't raise my hand. I wasn't going. I guess she wanted me to say it. So I did. "I am not going to the dance and I don't have a picture of me and my dad. As I anticipated, the class laughed. Stephanie proceeded to say "The only picture she has probably seen is his mug shot". Again the class laughed. But this time I was not going to let her get the best of me. I got out of my seat and charged Stephanie. I pushed her down and started pouncing on her. Mrs. Campbell was outraged at what was going on in her class. She said that she was disappointed in this behavior, but it was very obvious that what she really meant was that she was disappointed in my behavior. Instead of chastising both of us, she looked at me and said "young lady I will not tolerate this type of behavior in my class. She was forgetting that I was reacting to what Stephanie had said to me. If Stephanie had not said what she said, I would not have hit her.

Nevertheless, I knew that I would be punished. Mrs. Campbell decided that instead of sending me to the principal's office, she would handle it on her own, by making me work on the clean up committee at the father and daughter dance. I almost pleaded with her to just send me to the office and let me get that punishment that I was due. But for some reason, I changed my mind.

I might have convinced Michelle otherwise, but Marcus could see right through what I was saying. He told me "You told Michelle that you didn't want to go to the dance, but the truth is your pops don't want to take you. Don't anybody want to be seen with a fat pig. He laughed hysterically. Carl, a friend of mine, tried to defend me by telling him to give me a break and not to disrespect me by calling me names. But this only gave Marcus more ammunition to fight with.

The next day, we started class as usual with Mrs. Campbell calling the roll and giving us our assignments. The first thing that we were going to do was have an oral review of figurative language terms and then we would write about a topic in our journals. She started calling students on who sat on my row. She called Timothy and asked him what a simile was. Then she called on Sarah and asked her about metaphor. Finally, she was off my row, she skipped me. Whew, that was close. She called a few students on the first and second row and then that dreaded moment came, she called my name "Stacey". In a squeaky shaking voice, I said "yes ma'am. Mrs. Campbell asked" What is a hyperbole? All kinds of thoughts raced across my mind. I was sure that I knew what the answer was in my head, but why couldn't my mouth open to say it. I just gave her a blank stare and didn't say a mumbling word. I could still hear the echo of Mrs. Campbell's stern voice when she said "What is the matter, does the cat have your tongue? My mouth finally decides to cooperate with my brain and I managed to muster up a sound and I said "No". That's all I could come up with was "No". Is that the best that I could do and just say a simple word "No"? I started to beat myself up about it, but quickly remembered that I didn't need to because Mrs. Campbell was sure to do it. And beat me up was what she surely did. She did not beat with her hands, but rather with the tone of her voice and the words that she spoke. It was a verbal beating that I will remember for the rest of my life.

Mrs. Campbell said "No", is that all you have to say? "And why don't you know the answer"? Didn't you learn about types of figurative languages last year? This is last year's material, and you don't know it? What's the matter with you? Do you have a problem? I told Mrs. Campbell I don't have a problem? With the upmost confidence she said "Oh yes you have a problem. If you don't know this basic information by now, you have a problem. You must can't learn. That must be what it is, you can't learn. Class I finally figured out what Stacey's problem is, she can't learn. You are certainly not like your brother. Maybe you don't belong in here. Maybe you need to be in the special class.

I was humiliated beyond recognition. If I could have melted in my seat I would have. I could not believe that she had said those mean words to me especially in front of the boy that I have a crush on. What would he think about me now?

Mrs. Campbell transitioned us from oral review of figurative language to writing in our journals. This was my favorite part because I loved writing. I especially loved it when she didn't give us a topic and let us write about anything we wanted too. Well anything that was appropriate. But this time she gave us a topic, and it was "If you can have anything in the world that you want, it would be. She told us to begin writing. Some of the students in my class started writing while others were sitting pondering over what to write about. But not me, I immediately knew what I would write about. I wrote "If I could have anything in the world it would be a father that would love me and be proud of me. He would spend time with me and would celebrate with me when I did well. He would take time to listen to me. He would think that I was beautiful and make me feel special. My father would love me unconditionally and I would feel his love every day. With my daddy's love I could accomplish my dreams."

Fifteen minutes later. Mrs. Campbell told the class that it is time to stop writing. She asked for volunteers to share their journal entries. There was complete silence. Mrs. Campbell sarcastically said "Now don't you all volunteer all at one time". That still did not break the silence. I was praying that she did not call on me. But just as I was ending my prayer to God, I heard her say. "Ok Stacey, why don't you go first"?

I took a big swallow and a deep breath before I began to read my journal paper. I started "If I could be anything in the world, I mean if I could have anything in the world, it would be. I was trying to read as fast as I could. But the faster I tried to read, the more I stuttered and mumbled over my words. This was something that Mrs. Campbell did not like for students to do. She always said to read loud and clear so that everyone could understand what you were saying. I was sure that that would be the point that she would focus on, but to my surprise she didn't mention the way that I said my words, but rather she focused on what I said. After I read my paper, Mrs. Campbell stood up and said the most gut wrenching words to me "Of all the things that you could have chosen to write about and you chose to write about your father's love. Sweetheart, I am mighty afraid to tell you that if he doesn't love you by now, he'll never love you. There is nothing that you can do to make your father love you. You can't make anybody love you! The sooner you can accept that the better off you will be. Do you understand"?

At the time I did not understand why Mrs. Campbell would say that to me, but I found out later that her daddy had left her and her mama when she was a little girl. So she knew from experience the pain of growing up without a father's love. This made it even harder for me to understand why she would treat me the way that she did. Surely she understood what I was going through.

From that day on, I was open target for Mrs. Campbell to throw her fiery darts. It seemed that she found any way that she could to put me on the spot or make me feel uncomfortable. I was the first student that she called on to start our unit on impromptu speeches. With a smirk on her face, she called my name and told me to come to the front of the class. It was as if she already knew that I was going to mess up. She gave me a topic and told me to talk for 5 minutes. This had to be the longest five minutes in my life. The palms of my hands were sweaty and my knees were knocking together so loud that they had a rhythm of their own. My voice was shaking and I felt as if I was going to faint. I rocked back and forth trying to keep my balance. I fixated my eyes on a spot on the floor, trying to avoid making eye contact with anyone, especially with Mrs. Campbell.

To say that I hated speaking in front of the class is an understatement. I hated it with a passion. It showed that day when I stood before the class and Mrs. Campbell was sure to let me know just how bad I had messed up. It was time to stand before the great and mighty Mrs. Campbell to see what judgment she would cast on me. She stood and shouted "That was awful". In all of my many years of teaching, I have never seen anyone do as bad as that". You undoubtedly don't have the same genes as your brother. All I ever had to do was tell him what I expected of him, and he performed to my standards. What is your problem?

"If "you" people would spend your time and energy trying to learn something instead of fighting, maybe you would know the answer to the question that I am asking you. I guess I shouldn't expect anymore from you. This is usually how it is with children who don't have a father in their lives. They usually perform poorly in school and they seem to always be in trouble. It seems every year they put more and more of the trouble makers in my class. I should be so lucky".

The mockery that I experienced by both Mrs. Campbell and my father, made my self esteem cascade down to virtually nothing. Both gave me the clear indication that they did not approve of me and they certainly had very low expectations of me and my ability to be successful.

THE CONFRONTATION

Chapter 7

F OR THE FIRST TIME I cried in Mrs. Campbell's class. Like a scared little girl, I went home and told my mother what Mrs. Campbell had said. At first I wanted to add a little bit to the story to really get my mom fired up. One thing that I knew about my mom was that she didn't like anybody to bother her babies. But it was not necessary because my mom was already fired up. Out of all the things that Mrs. Campbell had said, the part that really stuck in my mom's mind was "you can't learn part". My mom did not seem too concerned about whether I really knew the answer or not or why I just said "no" or even the fact that I had not done well on my oral presentation. That was not as important to her as addressing the rude comment "you can't learn".

To my dad, Mrs. Campbell was right on target. He wholeheartedly agreed with every word that she had to say about me. He too thought that I lacked the capability of ever being smart and that I would be a statistic. He didn't give careful consideration of what Mrs. Campbell had said, because according to her, I would be a statistic because of his neglect. When my mom eluded to the fact that she was dismayed at what Mrs. Campbell had said to me and the way that she treated me, and that she intended to do something about it, my dad refused to subject himself to the humiliation of confronting authority figure on behalf of a daughter who was less than average.

The very next morning, my mom called my school to schedule a conference with Mrs. Campbell, Mr.Becktrim and Mr. Paulk, the school resource officer or SRO for short. I didn't quite understand why Mr. Paulk was invited to the meeting. Maybe he was there to keep everything in order or maybe he was going to arrest Mrs. Campbell. But I have never heard of a teacher being arrested for making rude comments, although it didn't sound like a bad idea, at least not for Mrs. Campbell anyway.

We all walked down the hallway that led to the conference room for the meeting. I could tell by the fast pace that my mom was walking and by the way she clutched her purse, that she was upset. I don't think that I have ever seen my mom so upset. Oh sure, I've seen the mad look in her eye if my brother or I misbehave in church or if we didn't do our best in school or if we are not truthful about something, but I have never seen her this furious. She sat across the table in perfect view of Mrs. Campbell. My heart was pounding so loud and hard I wondered in the back of my mind if anyone else could hear it. My mind began to wonder aimlessly about what my mom was going to say. I know that my mom is a good Christian lady, so I didn't expect her to curse at Mrs. Campbell, but the look on her face made it seem like she could. The conversation began with Mr. Becktrim saying "Mrs. Alexander, I understand that you have some concerns about something that supposedly happened in Mrs. Campbell's class". "No sir, it didn't supposedly happen, it did happen". Now Mrs. Campbell made some comments to my child and I don't appreciate it. I send my child to school to learn and get a good education and not to be put down because she doesn't know something", my mother said. I wondered if it would be a good time to interject and tell my mom that I really did know the answer I just couldn't get my mouth to work. I thought about it for a few brief seconds, and then I quickly dismissed the thought and decided to let mama continue. She was doing just fine without me. Mama continued, "I don't think any teacher has a right to tell a child that they can't learn. And she certainly does not have a right to compare her to her brother! She is who she is and her brother is who he is. They are two different people, each with their own good qualities. She is unique and according to what God's word says, she is wonderfully and fearfully made. And by the way, her father is a part of her life. He lives in the home with her.

Other parents may tolerate your attitude, but I will not. You don't have the right to put those negative thoughts in her mind. Now, I think you owe her an apology".

Mrs. Campbell took a few moments to digest everything that my mom had said, and then she finally voiced her opinion. "I am not going to apologize. You don't understand how difficult it is dealing with so many children. You need to face facts, that some kids are just slow learners. Unfortunately, that's what is mostly in my class this year. This is the worst teaching year that I have ever had. I don't think it is fair to me to have to deal with kids like this the whole year. I am accustomed to teaching gifted students. It is bad enough to have to teach average students, but to have to teach below average students, please". I don't have time to deal with a bunch of parents with high hopes for their children who clearly don't have the potential to be successful. And just so you know Mrs. Alexander, I took the liberty to check on Stacey's academic report and I see that she has been struggling since she has been in school. This is typical for children who don't have a positive male role model in lives. Statistics show that these type of kids struggle in school and have behavior problems. And just so you know just because her father lives in the home with her doesn't mean he is a part of her life. From the paper that she wrote in class, it would strongly suggest that he is clearly not a part of her life. Mrs. Alexander you seem to be in denial when it comes to your daughter. Now I have been teaching many years, and I see how children are affected by absent fathers. You say that he lives with her, but is he there for her emotionally? I might not know everything about your family but I know that your child is desperate for her father's love and attention". Trust me I know what it feels like to long for your father's love.

Mr. Becktrim stared in awe of everything that Mrs. Campbell had said. This was the first time I had ever seen Mr. Becktrim at a loss of words. But my mother certainly was not. She had a plenty to say. When my mother stood up it seemed as though she had grown another foot from the time when we came into the room. My mother pound her fist on the table and said at the top of her voice "what do you mean below average? My child is not a slow learner. She is very capable of learning, if you would just take the time to teach her. She has a gift and if you take the time to get to know her, you would see that. Don't tell me about a statistic. My baby is not and will not be a statistic! I don't know what she wrote in your class, but my family is just fine.

Without a doubt in my mind, I understood why Mr. Paulk was in the meeting, because things sure were getting heated. Mr. Becktrim finally recovered from his stupor condition and said "Ladies let's calm down". "Now I am sure that we can work something out. There has to be a solution to this problem". "Now Mrs. Alexander I understand that you are upset about the comment that was made, but I am sure that you are aware that all kids learn at a different pace. They don't all learn on the same level. Maybe your daughter needs some additional help. Obviously she didn't know the answer, so maybe this material is above her head. Maybe she" . . . . Without allowing him to finish his sentence, my mom interrupted and said "Don't you dare suggest that she be put in special education. If she needed, then that would be fine. I would be the first to suggest that she be put in Special Education. But this is not the case here. This boils down to a teacher who is used to having her way, and wants to pick and choose who she wants to teach instead of doing of her job and teaching whichever child walks through her classroom doors. I am so thankful that God is not like that. He has no respecter of person. He says come as you are. If God can accept all people, why can't you"?

The conversation kept going on, but I was still stuck on the possibility of me being in placed in Special Education. I thought to myself, "Oh no, I can't be in special education classes. What will all my friends think of me? Will they still want to be my friend? Will they think I am stupid?

Finally, I got up enough nerve and blurted out "I knew the answer, I just didn't say anything". In a synchronized pattern, they all asked "why didn't you answer the question, if you knew the answer?" I was afraid. I was afraid that if I really didn't know the answer like I thought I did, then Mrs. Campbell would be angry with me. I was afraid that Mrs. Campbell would yell at me if I didn't talk loud enough so everybody could hear me. I was paralyzed with fear. I just couldn't say anything.

For the very first time since the meeting had begun, there was complete silence. I tried to read the expressions on my mom, Mr.

Becktrim and Mrs. Campbell's face to try to decipher what they were thinking. But it was too late, my mom finally broke the silence and said the most dreadful thing "Mr. Becktrim, I am requesting that my daughter be removed out of Mrs. Campbell's class and be placed in Mrs. Davis class immediately.

"What?" What have I done? Put in another class, how could my mother let those words come out of her mouth? It was not that I liked being in Mrs. Campbell's class, but having to start over in a new class would be a lot worse, I think. And why did my mom have to say immediately, couldn't I wait until the end of the semester and then change classes? In my mind I wanted to ask this, but I knew that I had already talked way too much and besides when my mama said something that was how it was. That meeting took place on a Friday. That meant I had to spend the whole weekend thinking about being in a new class. This was sure to be the most tantalizing weekend ever. On Saturdays, after I do all of my chores, I usually ride my bicycle but this Saturday I didn't feel like it riding. I didn't feel like doing anything except writing in my journal. I spent all day Saturday in my room lying on my bed writing about everything that had happened and the anticipation of what school would be like on Monday. A part of me was happy that I was not in Mrs. Campbell's class, but starting over in another class made me feel scared.

That Sunday my mom and I got ready for church. She had decided to visit the church that was about two blocks away from our house. I liked this church okay but my mom liked it more than I did. She liked it because she thought that everyone was so nice, and to be honest they were. But I liked the other church on the other side of town better because most of my friends went to that church. I had pleaded with my mom for us to go to Camp Creek Baptist Church, but she insisted that we visit the church that she had chosen. She said that she felt led by the Holy Ghost to be present in their worship service that morning.

My mom and I arrived at church and as usual we sat on the front row. My mom always liked to sit on the front row. It did not matter what church she was attending, she would always find a space on the front row. That would be okay, except she felt the need to drag me along with her. I didn't complain about too many things when it came to going to church, but having to sit on the front row was one of the things that I did complain about. I asked my mom why we couldn't sit somewhere else. She would always say that she sit on the front row to be closer to the fire. She wanted to be as close to the pulpit to make certain that she didn't miss a word that Rev. Smith was saying.

As I was listening to the preacher, I heard him say that God has not given us the spirit of fear, but of power and of love and of a sound mind. He said that no matter what situation that you are facing, if you trust God he will take you through. Then he said, "the key is you have to trust God". I remember thinking to myself, can I really trust God? He closed his sermon with "God will help you conquer any fear". I meditated on those seven words that the preacher said; "God will help you conquer any fear". Then I can remember whispering a small prayer to God, Will you take away my fear? I didn't feel any real significant change. I wasn't even sure if God heard me. Why would God want to listen to me? After all, I was the one who got myself into this situation, not God. If only I had answered the question in the first place, I would not have been in this situation.

GRANDMA'S HOUSE

Chapter 8

ONE OF OUR FAVORITE PASTIMES was to go to my grandmother's house every Sunday. Usually we would go to her house after church. My grandmother loved to cook, and it made her feel good to see people enjoy eating her food. She would always have a big smile on her face, as people from all walks of life ushered in to be seated around her dining room table. She would always cook enough food with the intent of feeding the whole neighborhood.

My grandmother's house was a safe haven. It seemed that no matter what a person was going through, no matter how bad it was she would always have a word from God to encourage you. She would say "Baby everything is going to be alright, just trust God". Being at my grandmother's house was sure to take everything off my mind about going to a new class and having to miss the Father / Daughter dance.

Marcus was right I did want to go to the Father/ Daughter dance and it showed in my face. My grandmother could always tell when something was wrong with me. She pulled me to the side and said "I want to talk to you. Why are you looking so down? "Don't you know that you can't let anything get you down? I know that you are upset about what your teacher said about you. People will always have their own opinion about you, but that doesn't make it right. You are special and God is going to use you for His glory. Everything is going to be alright. God will always take care of you. I brought your mama up trusting the Lord, now I want you to do the same. This family always

41

has and always will trust the Lord. We don't fear anything because we know that we got God on our side.

Now what's going on between you and your dad? What's this I hear about you talking about you wished your daddy was dead? I shouted to her, "He might as well be. He does not ever want to spend time with me. He does not to be a part of my life. Sometimes I wish . . . . She interrupted me and stopped me from finishing what I going to say. She told me that no matter what my dad did or did not do, she told me that I had to respect him as my dad. She told me to pray for my dad that God would change him. She always encouraged me to not to give up on my dad. To be honest, there were times that I was so discouraged that I wanted to give up. I had prayed for him and things had not changed. She told me to keep praying and not to worry because God would work everything out in his own time.

Yes ma'am I said. I gave her a big smile and hug. I felt so much better. It was as if a ton of bricks were lifted off my chest. I could finally relax my mind and be at peace.

I was ready to eat some of my grandmother's good ole soul food. We had fried chicken, ham, potato salad, macaroni and cheese, corn, collard and turnip greens corn bread, sweet potatoes and peach cobbler, sweet potato pie and ice tea. I always looked forward to eating at my grandmother's house.

Although my grandmother had extended an invitation to anyone who wanted to come and eat, Ms. Gertrude would always come with her own agenda. It seemed that Ms. Gertrude could sense the exact time that we were about to sit down and start to eat because she always managed to come just at the right time. She would come with the same lame excuse, "Oh I see you all about to eat, and I don't want to disturb you so I guess I better go on home. My grandmother would always follow by saying "Oh you know you are welcome to eat here. We got plenty, come on and help yourself". I felt like saying, "yes, why don't you go home". But I know that both my mom and my grandmother would think that I was being rude. Ms. Gertrude didn't come just to eat, but she also came to give the latest gossip. She acquired the nickname, Gossiping Gertrude, because she gossiped about everybody. Everyone knew that if you ever wanted to know about somebody else's business, just ask Ms. Gertrude because she was sure to know. Gossip was one thing that my grandmother did not allow in her house, which was why I couldn't understand why she would allow her to come over every Sunday. Ms. Gertrude came to the dinner table and started to fix her plate. Then she started telling us the latest news. She started talking about how she didn't like Rev. Smith's sermon last Sunday. She said he didn't preach good and he was off his game. She confessed that she didn't put any money in the offering plate because she didn't get fed. Her motto was that she only pays for her meal that she eats; since she didn't get anything out of Rev. Smith's sermon she didn't give any money.

She moved on from Rev. Smith and started talking about how short Sister Mary's skirt was. She concluded that Sister Mary short skirt was probably the reason that Rev. Smith didn't preach well. He couldn't focus on his message trying so hard to look at Sis. Mary's legs. In between taking a bite of chicken and drinking her tea, she managed to announce that Bro. James is drinking again and his wife was thinking about leaving him. As if that wasn't enough, my aunt Trella joined in, she said, "well tell me this, is Sandra and her husband back together?

My grandmother finally intervened, and said "Now you all know better. You are not supposed to be talking about folks. The truth be told, we all need help in some kind of way. We are supposed to build people up and not tear people down.

Soon Ms. Gertrude left and went back home. She never volunteered to wash a single dish or even sweep the floor. I was glad when she left. It was as if a cloud of darkness disappeared when she left. The whole atmosphere changed in the house.

It was about time for us to leave my grandmother's house and go home, but just before we could leave, I heard my Aunt Trella call my mom to the back of the room. Normally, I would have been glad that she was holding us up from going home because this meant more time that I could spend with my cousins, but this time it was different. I was intrigued to know what Aunt Trella had to say to my mom. My aunt Trella had a certain look in her eye, as if she was up to something and I wanted to know what it was. My mom told Aunt Trella that she only had a few minutes because we had to get home so we could get our things ready for the next day.

My mom walked in the room with Aunt Trella and she closed the door behind her. Just above a whisper, I could hear my Aunt Trella ask my mom about her relationship with my dad. As always, my mom gave her usual reply, "everything is alright". My mom knew full well that everything was not alright between her and my dad. Aunt Trella knew better, she told my mom I know things are not alright between you and Michael. Michael is not treating you right and he sure is not treating Stacey like a father should. I don't understand how you can keep putting up with his mess. He never spends any time with you or Stacey. He is so mean. My mom interrupted my Aunt Trella, and told her that was over stepping her boundaries and that was enough talking about her husband. He may not be all that he can be but nobody is perfect. Aunt Trella apologized for getting my mom upset and then she changed the subject and tried to talk about something that would make my mom laugh. Aunt Trella said "Girl, I saw your old main squeeze, and he is looking fine too". My mom gave a little chuckle and she asked "Who are you talking about? Aunt Trella said "You know who I am talking about!!!! I am talking about Frank Simmons, your old sweetheart. Girl, I know you hate Michael made you quit your job. I know you miss seeing those tight abs every day". He undoubtedly had to be special if my Aunt Trella was talking about him now especially after my mom and my dad had been married for so many years. I made my cousins go back in the front room, so I could hear everything that they were saying. I heard Aunt Trella say to my mom, "You remember how crazy he was about you. He used to say that if you two ever got married that you all would have a house full of children and he would be there to take care of them all. He sure did love children." "Yes he did love children, and the children loved him" said Rebecca. "He was a good man", both Aunt Trella and my mom said together. They both laughed. Aunt Trella said He has a good job he's the owner of Frank's Auto Shop and he is in the church too. I remember he used to get on my nerves always talking the names that he was going to name his children. Remember how he would talk about how if he had a daughter, how he would treat her like a princess and do special father/daughter things together like take her to the Father/ Daughter dance. Yes, I remember that, my mom said.

Then Aunt Trella asked my mom "Is Michael going to take Stacey?" My mom got upset, and told my aunt that she had to go. I quickly ran to the front of the room with the cousins. I could tell the look on my mom's face that she was upset. She grabbed me by arm and told me "come on, let's go home". My Aunt Trella, kept saying I'm sorry, I didn't mean to upset you.

The ride home was quiet, my mom didn't say a word and neither did I. I don't know if she was thinking about what Aunt Trella had, but I sure was. I was thinking about Mr. Frank Simmons. I calculated a plan in my mind about how I could meet him and for a brief moment I thought maybe he just maybe he would want to take me to the Father/ Daughter dance.

MY FIRST FATHER/ DAUGHTER DANCE

Chapter 9

I HAD HEARD MY AUNT TRELLA say that Mr. Frank owned Frank's Auto Shop and I desperately wanted to meet him. But I did not know what I would say to him. I couldn't very well just go to him and just ask him to take me to Father/ Daughter Dance. I know that my Aunt Trella said that he was nice and he loved children, but what if he has changed. What if he doesn't like children anymore? Better yet, what if he has children of his own, and he doesn't have time for any other kids? What if he asks about my father, what would I tell him about my father? What if he could see what my father sees in me that makes him not love me? What if Mr. Frank doesn't like me either?

I tossed those and a few more "what if questions" in my mind, but then I realized that this is something that I had to do. I had to meet Mr. Frank Simmons for myself. I made up my mind that I would go and pay him a visit Monday after school. I had told my mom that I was staying after school for a club meeting. She had given me permission to stay after school for the club meeting, but she definitely did not give me permission to go and see Mr. Frank Simmons. I am quite sure if she knew what I was doing she would be disappointed, and would prohibit me from going, that is why I didn't tell her. This is something that I had to do for myself. This could be my only shot at having a real male role model in my life. I didn't want to miss my opportunity.

Immediately after the school bell rang, I walked to Frank's Auto Shop. I was mesmerized by all the cars he had on his lot. I must have looked at what seems like a 100 cars. I loved them all, but favorite was Mercedes Benz SLK350. It was sleek and shiny red. I had my forehead placed against the driver's side window, looking inside at the leather seats and all the gadgets that control everything. It was fascinating. I was visualizing myself driving that car then all of sudden, I felt someone tap me on my shoulder. I was startled by a short, dark skin, man with a puzzled look on his face who looked down at me and said "You look mighty young to be drive, so I know that you didn't come here to buy a car. Trying to get my composure, I said No sir, I didn't come to buy a car". I was just looking". He laughed and in turn said, "Well looking at car and buying cars are two different things. I can't make any money if you just look. Tell you what when you get ready to buy a car, you come back then. I just looked and said "Ok". That was not the reason that I went to the car lot. I went to meet Mr. Frank Simmons. I had missed this opportunity for now, but I knew that I could not give up.

Three days passed by, and I decided that I would give it another try. This time I would be prepared and no matter what I would meet Mr. Frank Simmons. I went to the car lot, this time I went inside of the shop that way I would not get caught up looking at the cars. As I walked in a man stopped me and asked me where was I headed because I need to be with an adult? He asked where were my parents? I informed him that I was alone and my parents were not with me. He tried to explain to me why children needed to be with their parents and why children needed to be supervised and something about the cars there being very expensive and unsupervised children might damage the cars. He said a lot more, but all I could hear in my mind was "You can't meet Mr. Frank Simmons". That was all that I heard in my mind. I had yet another obstacle standing in my way keeping me from completing my mission.

I did not know what I was going to do, but I knew that I had to meet him. I walked all the way home thinking how I was going to meet Mr. Frank Simmons. I knew that I couldn't give up. Then all of a sudden it came to me. I would do what I like doing the best and that is to write. I decided that I would write him a letter. In my letter I told him that I had been given an assignment to interview a successful black business owner and that I had heard a lot about him and that I wanted to interview him. Of course this was not actually an assignment, but I figured who could say no if it would help get a good education. I gave the letter to the man who had stopped me before and asked that he give the letter to Mr. Frank Simmons.

Two days later I went to Mr. Frank's shop to meet him. As I enter the door, the man who had stopped me before was there. He led me to Mr. Frank's office. I finally got a chance to meet him. He looked just the way Aunt Trella had described him. He was a tall, bright skin, man with broad shoulders, with hazy brown hair, silky black eyes and a big smile on his face. Just based on his looks, I could tell why Aunt Trella was rant and raving about him. He reached out and shook my hand, and told me to come into his office. He did his best to clear the mountain of paperwork on his desk and then he offered me a soda. I gladly accepted the soda and we began what he thought was a school interview. I began by asking him about his business. How long had he been in business? How did he decide to go into the car business? For every business question that I asked, I asked a personal question. I wanted to know if he had a family. Did he have children? Did he want to have children? I was firing questions so fast that he had to stop me so he could catch his breath. I asked him all kinds of questions and he in turned asked me questions about myself. He wanted to know what school I attended. He asked about my grades in school. What things that I was interested in? He was concerned about the things that were going on in my life.

This interview was supposed to be about him, but it turned out that I was the one who was sharing the most about my life. It was so easy to talk to him. He didn't seem to mind listening to me talk. He made me feel like I was important. I convinced him that I needed to come back the next day to finish the interview. He agreed to let me come back. Over the next three weeks, I came back to his shop and we continued to talk and the more we talked the more we found out about each other. I shared with him about my love for writing and my dream to one day publish a book. Unlike my dad, he seemed very intrigued about my goal to become a published author. I told him that my dad did not believe that I would ever be a successful writer because it took special people to write books. In my dad's eyes, I was not special. Mr. Frank thought differently, he believed that I had what it took to be a successful author and he knew in his heart that I was special. He believed that I could do anything that I set my mind to. To prove that he believed in me, he eventually offered me a part time job helping him keep his paperwork organized, so I could earn money to save to have my book published. I was happy going to work every day. I liked being around Mr. Frank and I could tell that he liked being around me.

There was one day that I went to work and I wasn't in my chipper mood that I usually am. Just like any loving and attentive father would be able to pick up, Mr. Frank could automatically tell that something was wrong with me. He asked was I okay? I explained to him that the Father Daughter dance was going to be held that night and my father was not going to take me. To make matters worse, as a punishment for the trouble that I had gotten into at school, I had to serve on the cleaning committee at the Father/ Daughter dance. I expressed my concern about being humiliated when the other girls saw me there without my father let alone working on the cleaning committee. Mr. Frank continued to listen to me, then as always he tried to reassure me that everything would be okay and that something good would come out of this. I could not see anything good coming out of this situation at all.

I continued to work and I heard Mr. Frank tell his receptionist to hold all of his calls and he left his office for the day. He usually did not leave his office early unless there was something urgent that he had to take care of. I did not know of any meetings that he had scheduled so I could not think of any reason why he would leave early.

I finished my job for the day and then I went home so I could prepare to go to the Father Daughter dance. I told my mom that I was going to the dance as one of my club requirements; I didn't dare tell her that it was a punishment. I would have been in more trouble than I cared to deal with.

The time had finally come to go to the dance. On my way there, I tried to convince myself that everything would be okay, that I would survive the night. As I entered the ballroom, I saw some of the decorations had already been put up on the walls. I saw a sign that read "Father Daughter Dance". I saw the wall with the pictures of the girls and their dad. Then I saw the red carpet where the dads escorted their daughters down the middle aisle to have their pictures taken.

I was looking around admiring how beautiful our school cafeteria had been transferred into an elegant ballroom, and in the corner of my eye I saw someone who I thought looked just like Mr. Frank Simmons. To my surprise, it was Mr. Frank Simmons. He was dressed in a black tuxedo with a red cummerbund. He had a garment bag lying over his arm. I asked him what he was doing there and he said that he was there to be my escort. He handed me the garment bag and told me to go and change my clothes. He had left work early to go to Unique Boutique to buy me a dress to wear to the dance. I don't know if I more amazed of the fact that he would actually take the time to do something so nice as this or the fact that he actually knew that much about me that he could go and shop for me and actually pick something that I like.

With the biggest smile on my face, I ran in the back and changed my clothes. I walked out and everybody including Mrs. Campbell clapped for me. Mr. Frank gave me a look that signified his approval, he said "Beautiful, Absolutely beautiful. You look like a princess. To be honest, I felt like a princess. Mr. Frank was right; something good did come out of this situation. I never wanted this night to end.

The photographer walked up to Mr. Frank and asked if he could take a picture of him and his daughter. He didn't bother to correct him and tell him that I was not his daughter; he just simply laughed and said "sure".

Not that I minded at all, but I asked him why he didn't tell the photographer that I was not his daughter. He looked at me and said "You think I am going to disown the most beautiful young lady at the dance. I'm not crazy. Now may I have this dance? I smiled and held my hand out. Mr. Frank grabbed and we danced together. The photographer took some more pictures of us, but he was not the only one. I saw my uncle Jim in the corner talking to a young lady who was three times younger than he was. He had been drinking. He managed to take the time to stagger over and make me aware of presence. He was very inquisitive about why I was at the dance with

Mr. Frank instead of my dad. He wanted to know if my dad knew that I was on a date. I was honest to say that I was not on a date and that my dad did not know that I was there. Maybe if I had said yes he knew then maybe he would have left well enough alone and went on and minded his own business. But instead he kept badgering me. He was trying to hug me and blowing kisses at me. After I had had enough, Mr. Frank got in my uncle's face and told him that he was going to ask only once that he go away and leave me alone. Of course my uncle took offense to this; he repeatedly took pictures of me and Mr. Frank. He walked up to me with a day old beer breath, with a vindictive voice he said "don't worry your secret is safe with me". I just hope that I don't have to use these pictures.

THE BEST OF TIMES/
THE WORST OF TIMES

Chapter 10

GOING TO THE DANCE WAS the highlight of my life. I finally understood what people meant when they said that they were on cloud nine. This was how I felt; like I was on cloud nine. What Mr. Frank had done for me would be a memory that would be etched on the crevices of my brain for an eternity. He had gone the extra mile just to make me feel special.

This happiness that I felt was very short lived. Troubling times lied ahead for me. Tragedy after tragedy took place. My whirlwind of problems began when my grandmother got sick. I can remember sitting in my room writing in my journal, when I heard the phone ring. It sounded louder than usually, as if it was trying to warn us that trouble was on the other end. My mom answered the phone. She listened as my Aunt Bee told her about my grandmother. She wasn't saying a word, just listening as my aunt talked. I couldn't help but think, what was wrong. Why wasn't she saying anything? I came to end of the hallway so I could hear if my mom was going to say anything. Finally, my mom broke her silence. She told my dad that my grandmother had had a stroke and the doctors didn't think that she was going to make it. I ran out of my room and grabbed my mama, with tears in my eyes, I said "Mama what are we going to do? We can't make it without Grandmother. My mother looked at me and said "hush child, now is not the time for you to be carrying on. We are going to do what we always do. Pray. Pray to God, child. He is the only one who can help any of us". My mind kept rehearsing what the doctor had said "she may not make it", but then I thought about what my grandmother always said, just because somebody says something about you doesn't make it true. She said "God always have the final say in every situation".

Frantically, my mama got her coat and purse and was headed to the door. My dad stormed out of the kitchen looked at her, and said with his loud thunderous voice, "Where do you think you are going"? I am going to the hospital, I have to go and take care of my mama, my mama said.

"What about me? I been working all day you need to stay home and to take care of me. Besides you know that I have diabetes and I have to eat at a certain time. I have to be taken care of first. You can't go now, not until you take care of my needs. Why are always the first one that your family calls anyway. You ain't God. Why can't they go? You don't have to be at that hospital, that's what they have doctors for. The last time I checked, you were not a doctor".

I couldn't believe what my dad was saying. How could he stoop so low to try to stop my mama from going to see her own mama? How could he be so mean? My dad kept yelling at my mom, making comments about her being a church going woman and how she should be able to pray from anywhere. In a very sarcastic way, he said" I thought you said that it don't matter where you are when you pray, God can hear you from anywhere" Well if he can hear you from anywhere why do you have to go the hospital, pray from home. Then he burst out into an evil high pitched laugh. My grandmother used to tell me about how people let the devil use them to do evil; this must have what she was talking about.

I couldn't take it anymore; I interjected my two senses and told my dad that he was just being selfish and that Grandma Mattie needed us more than he did. He looked at me with such a discussing look and said that my mother could go but I had to stay home to fix him something to eat. I pleaded with him to let both of us go. But he would not agree to it. He was insistent that I stay home. All I could think about what if something happened to Grandma Mattie and I was not there. I did not want to stay home and fix food for my dad; the last thing that I wanted to do was be nice to him considering the way he was acting. I could not understand how or why my dad would be so mean especially during a time like this. I was angry with my dad. My place should have been by Grandma Mattie's side not stuck at home doing something that he was fully capable of doing for himself. My heart's desire was to be there with Grandma Mattie. Why couldn't he understand that?

My mom left and went to the hospital. She later told me that when she got there, my Aunt Bee, Aunt Mary, and Aunt Trella were all standing around my grandmother's bed. They all ran to my mother and began to cry. Executing her authority as their older strong sister, my mother looked at them, and "oh no, we are not going to handle this situation like this. Now get yourselves together, and stop all that crying, it's praying time". They all joined hands and my mother prayed.

Just like my grandmother, my mother was known to pray about everything. I would often hear people in our community and in our church tell my mom about problems that they were having or about somebody who was sick. And my mom would give her usual response "I'll be praying for them. And she did. She prayed for everybody even my dad. That was one thing that I did not understand. Why would my mom be nice and pray for my dad and he definitely was not nice to her and her certainly was not praying for her. I jokingly asked her, "What was wrong with you mama"? She laughed and said "there ain't a thing wrong with me child. That is how Jesus wants us to be. He wants us to show love to people, even if they don't show love to us". I didn't say this to my mama, but if she had asked me, I would have told her that she was just wasting a prayer praying for my daddy. I felt that there was no hope for him.

It had been a couple of hours since my mom had left home to go to the hospital to see my grandmother. After what seemed like an eternity, she finally came home. I met her at the door, gave her a big hug and a kiss and asked about my grandmother. She said that her condition had been stabilized and she was able to move from ICU to her own hospital bed. She was resting and would be fine. I was so relieved. I couldn't imagine life without my grandmother.

My grandmother stayed in the hospital for 3 weeks and was finally being discharged to come home. The next couple of weeks were trying times for all of us, especially for my grandmother. We are excited and grateful that she was coming home, but we also knew that she was going to need a lot of help. My mom had told me that things were going to be different from the way they used to be, and that I should do all that I could to help my grandmother in any way that she needed me. I was prepared to do whatever she wanted me to do. I was determined that I was going to stay by her side and nobody was going to stop me and that included my father.

After seeing my grandmother for the first since she had had the stroke, I realized that things would never be the same. Most of the things that my grandmother used to do, she could no longer do. She was not able to prepare Sunday meals like she used to and she couldn't work in her garden. The right side of her body was affected so she would have to endure months of rehabilitation.

I remember how aggravated that she would get because she couldn't communicate to us way she wanted to. It was frustrating because she had to write whatever she wanted to say on a notepad. Things were definitely different, and although I was grateful to have her, I missed the way she once was. I missed hearing her voice.

It was exactly six months later when my grandmother had her 2nd stroke. I remember when my Aunt Trella called my mom and told her to come to the hospital because my grandmother was sick. This time I convinced my mama to let me go with her. When we arrived at the hospital, I saw my all family. My aunts, my uncles and my cousins were all standing around. Some of them were crying. I thought to myself, why are they crying didn't they believe that Grandmama Mattie was going to be all right? I sure did believe that she was going to be alright. I thought that it would just like the last time. She would be in the hospital maybe for the couple of weeks and then she would go home. We would come together as a family and help take care of her. I really believed that was how it was going to be.

But as I approached my grandmother's room, I had a sick feeling in the bottom of my stomach and my heart began to race. It felt like a 100 miles per hour. I pushed the door open and saw my grandmother lying there hooked up to a machine. I later found out that this machine was helping her to breathe. She had tubes in her nose and her mouth. My mom came in my grandmother's room and in a rough tone, she said "Lord, just look at my mama". Shortly after the doctor walked in and said that he needed to talk to the family. He sat us all down and looked in each of our eyes and told us "that he had done all that he could, but it just didn't look good. There is too much swelling around her brain. I don't think she will make it through the night". I couldn't believe what I was hearing. It was like my whole world stood still. What did he mean she won't make it through the night? Who was he to say? He wasn't God. Grandma Mattie always said that God has the final say.

My mama thanked the doctor and told him that she was going to keep praying. My mom stayed in the room, but I left and went to the waiting room with the rest of my family. We all joined hands and prayed that my grandmother would be healed. After praying, I felt a sense of hope that just maybe my grandmother would pull through. I waited expecting to hear some good news about my grandmother, that God had performed miracle and she was going to be all right again. But that was not what happened. My mother came to the waiting room, and told us that my grandmother's respirations were slowing down and that we should go see her. I could tell by the tone of my mother's voice things were not good with my grandmother. We each went in to see her in pairs. My Trella aunt and her husband went first. It was few minutes later and my aunt and uncle came out and she said told me that I could go in to see my grandmother. I went into her room and held her hand. In that brief moment I had a flashback to the times that I spent with my grandmother. I thought about some of the things that she had taught me. I could her hear telling me "to always trust God".

THE MISSING LINK

Chapter 11

Two hours later, my grandmother passed away. This was the most devastating thing that I have ever experienced in my life. Her death seemed so surreal. The indescribable pain that I felt in my heart was too much for me to bear. I felt like a black cloud of hopelessness, hung over my head and that I was never going to recover from this tragedy. Trying to figure out my place in the world now, and learning how to cope with my grandmother's death, I sank myself into my favorite past time; writing. I meditated on the pain and the cold facts of how life would be now and pulled it up to the surface of my heart, and I begin to write.

Dear Diary,

Today was the most gruesome day of my life. I can't imagine living life without my grandmother. She was my best friend. This is it. I can't take it anymore.

Over the next couple of days, my mom and my aunts made preparations for my grandmother's funeral. They did all the things that come along with planning a funeral, like writing the obituary, deciding what she would wear to be buried in and who would do the eulogy. They decided that the funeral would be Saturday May 4th at 2:00.

I told my mother that I didn't want to go to my grandmother's funeral. I think a part of me wanted to remember her as she was. Maybe my subconscious was fooling me into thinking that if I didn't go the funeral that Grandma Mattie's death wouldn't be real. It might sound crazy, but in my mind it made sense. I was willing to do anything to numb the pain of losing my best friend.

On the day of my grandmother's funeral, it was cold and raining, just the opposite of the kind of weather that she liked. I imagined in my mind, seeing her in the yard planting seeds for collard greens, turnip greens, okra and corn. It was hard to stretch my mind to envision seeing her lying lifeless in her casket.

The funeral home director came to my grandmother's house, and escorted me and all of my family members to the limousine. My Aunt Dee and her husband, Uncle Jim rode in the front seat and my mom and I rode in the back seat. It seemed to take forever to get to the church, not that I was in any hurry to get there. I rode with my forehead smashed against the car window looking as the rain came pouring out of the sky. Maybe I should have put my arms around my mom and comforted her, but at the time I didn't think about it. To be honest, I didn't have the strength to comfort anyone, not even myself. Oh the pain was definitely there, and I could feel it deep down in my soul, but I just didn't know what to do with the pain. That is what I mean by I couldn't comfort myself. Besides this was my father's job. He should have been there to comfort my mom.

As we approached the church, I could feel a big lump in my throat and tears in my eyes. I walked slowly in the church trying to prolong the inevitable, and embrace the fact that this would be the final time seeing my grandmother. As I was walking my mind went back to all the times I had seen my grandmother shouting and giving God the praise. I thought about all the Sunday meals that she had cooked for the church. She never asked for anything in return. She always said that she did what she did from her heart. I believed that too because my grandmother had the biggest heart.

As I was walking in, I counted the empty seats. They were the empty seats that I thought should have been filled with the people who claimed all along that they loved her. Besides our family, there were only enough people to fill half of the church. As much as my grandmother had done for all the people in her church and her community, I couldn't understand why every seat in that church was not filled. I thought about all the meals that she had cooked for people who were hungry and didn't have food and even for those who were just too lazy to cook. As many prayers as she had prayed for people, that church should have been full. Now there were flowers galore. I bet there were twice as many flowers as there were people. If there were as many people as there were flowers, the church would have been overfilled. I guess the flowers were from the people who didn't think enough of her to come and pay their respect. There were some who were genuine and made remarks about my grandmother that reflected that, but there were also some there who came as spectators. I knew this because I overheard Ms. Laura say "They sure did a good job on her. She looked just like herself". I wanted to say "Well who does she suppose to look like?"

I was so angry because the love and time that my grandmother had invested in so many lives, obviously was not appreciated. I thought to myself, is this what Christian love looks like? Is this the way that Christians are suppose to treat one another? More importantly I wondered who would carry on her legacy of demonstrating her unwavering faith and the unconditional love that she had for everyone and her ability to bring out the best of everyone.

I sat on the front seat between my mother and my Aunt Trella. I lost total control of my emotions all at once. I was sad because I knew that I would never see my grandmother again. There would be no more family gatherings. When I had problems I would not have my grandmother to talk to. I was also mad because in my mind, my grandmother didn't deserve to die. She was the sweetest God fearing woman that I knew. I couldn't understand why God would let my grandmother die and let other people who didn't even go to church live. My grandmother was dedicated to serving God and taking care of the church. I also felt a sense of relief because now I know that my grandmother was not suffering and in so much pain. That was the only relief that I had. Now she didn't have to be so frustrated about having to write down everything that she wanted to say because nobody could understand her when she tried to talk.

I sat there starring at my grandmother casket. She didn't belong in there. Even if no one else seemed to care, I still cared. She still had some more prayers to pray. She still had some more advice to give me. This wasn't fair.

I was grieving the loss of my grandmother. There was such an empty void in my life that I did not know how to fill. My mom tried to reach out to me but she could not help me because she was grieving too. I couldn't help but wonder where was my daddy in all of this? Every girl needs her daddy when she is hurting. He was not there to tell me what to do with all this pain. How do I live through the turmoil that I was facing? I know that it was not my dad's fault that Grandma Mattie was not here with us anymore, but it was his fault that he did not open up to us. Through the whole ordeal he had a nonchalant attitude, as if he didn't care. I couldn't seem to get past that.

THE ULTIMATE BETRAYAL

Chapter 12

Aᶠᵗᵉʳ ᵗʰᵉ ᵖᵃˢˢⁱⁿᵍ ᵒᶠ ᵐʸ grandmother, my Uncle Jim took a special interest in me. He said he knew how close Grandma Mattie and I were and he knew that I was sad about losing her and he wanted to help me get over it. Then he talked about my relationship with my dad not being good and how he wanted to be that special male role model in my life. He had noticed that my dad was not lending his support in helping me deal with this situation. He said that if I needed anything just let him know and he would get it for me. This totally caught me by surprise because my uncle usually didn't say very much to me, but what he said was music to my ears. I had already lost the closest thing to having genuine love in my life when my grandmother passed away, so you better believe I took advantage of his offer. I thought maybe this was another shot at being loved again.

It was a week or so later after our conversation that Aunt Dee and Uncle Jim invited me to go out to dinner with them. Uncle Jim was sure to let me know that it was perfectly okay for me to order anything that I wanted. As if it was exciting enough to be out for dinner, but I could order anything that I wanted. My family rarely went out to eat because my daddy didn't like to eat at restaurants so we usually ate my mom's home cooked meals.

After we each placed our orders, Aunt Dee had to step in the lobby of the restaurant to make a phone call. I don't know who she had to call, but apparently it had to be important. While Uncle

Jim and I sat waiting on our meals to be served we engaged in a conversation about the things that I liked to do in my spare time, and of course boys. He wanted to know if a pretty girl like me had a lot of boyfriends, what did I find attractive in a boy, if I had ever kissed a boy or if I would ever consider dating an older man? Perhaps this conversation that should have sent up a red flag, but at the time it did not register with me that it could be viewed as inappropriate. It was after I told him that one of the things that I liked to do in my spare time was to watch basketball on television that he promised to take me to a professional basketball game. From that point, I completely dismissed our conversation. I love basketball and was content with just watching on television. But to have an opportunity to see a game live and in person was a dream come true. I had seen many college basketball teams play on television, but I always wanted to go a big arena and see how the professionals play basketball. I was finally getting my chance to go.

Just as I had imagined, it was so much fun. After the game we went out to eat at a nice restaurant. This was a night that I would remember for the rest of my life. From that point on, every weekend either Aunt Dee or Uncle Jim would call to see if I wanted to hang out with them. I loved spending time with the both of them. I enjoyed every minute of it.

Everything was going good until my aunt started asking me to babysit. My uncle would come to our house and ask my mama if I could come to their house because my aunt Trella wanted me to babysit my little cousins. My mama would always "yes, that will give her something to do, keep her out of trouble". My uncle would come alone to pick me up. At first that as okay, but over time he began to do things to me that I knew couldn't be right. The things that he was doing made me feel uncomfortable riding with him. As soon, as I would get in the car, he would smile and tell me how beautiful I was. He would compliment me about my clothes and how good I looked in them. Then he would grab and kiss the back of my hand. He would rub my thighs and laugh while he was doing it. I thought maybe if I looked straight ahead and tried not look at him, just maybe he wouldn't say anything to me. Maybe he wouldn't try to touch me. But this strategy never worked.

When we got to his house, my aunt would always make a comment like ""Jim hasn't been aggravating you have he? Or Jim has been behaving himself hasn't he? It was almost as if she knew something was going on. This would have been the perfect time to tell her that something really was going on, but instead I just would give her a little smirk, I guess signaling to her that everything was okay. But everything was not okay.

Every time that my uncle would come and ask my mama if I could babysit she would say the same thing. "Yes, it will give her something to do and keep her out of trouble". Oh how I was hoping that one day my mom would say no that I couldn't babysit. But she never did.

What she didn't realize was that I was already in trouble. My uncle continued to touch me. There were so many times when my aunt would leave to go to work, that my uncle would try to lure me into his bedroom. I would tell him that I did not want to go into his bedroom, but he would insist that I come. If he didn't think that I was moving fast enough, he would come and grab and drag me into his bedroom. He would push me on the bed, and lay his 285 lb body on top of my frail 110 lb body, and he tried to have sex with me. But somehow I muster up enough strength to fight him off. I intentionally made a lot noises to make my cousins come in the room. This would make my uncle so mad. Mad enough to take me home for that time, but not mad enough to stop doing what he was doing. This happened for year and as time went by things got progressively worse.

With suppressed memories of having to fight him off of me, I did everything that I could to pretend that everything was okay. I didn't want anyone to know about what was going on. The only person that I trusted with my secret was my friend Tina. I made her promise to never tell anyone. To my knowledge, she never did. As much as I loved my mother, I couldn't find the strength to tell her. My uncle would always tell me that if I told, my family would all be hurt, especially her mom. I didn't want to hurt her mom, or anybody in her family for that matter, so I just kept quiet about it all. That is exactly what my uncle wanted me to do. As long as he was not being exposed about the wrong that he was doing, he was able to continue to do what he did. A part of me felt that it was my fault because I continued to let it go on. I told him to stop and I made it perfectly clear to him that I did not like what he was doing to me, but I didn't have enough courage to tell anybody else except Tina. Maybe if I had said something, maybe the other kids in my neighborhood would not have gone through the same thing that I went through.

But it was too late. One day I overheard my mom and father talking about Uncle Jim. There had been some talk about him trying to have sex with some of the other girls that were my same age. I remember my mom saying, "I don't know if it is true, but if it is, that is a shame. I don't know what I would do if that ever happened to Stacey". A big lump welled up in my throat and a sick feeling sat in the pit of my stomach.

Forced against my will, I told my mother that Uncle Jim had tried to have sex with me on several occasions. That moment my whole world changed. There was a sigh of relief that I no longer had to keep the secret but it also was a disgrace because I had hurt my mother. I could see the hurt look in my mother's eyes. What must have been going through her mind? Was she ashamed of me? Was I a disgrace to her? Did she believe what I was saying? My mother looked in my eyes and asked me "Why didn't you tell me?" I looked at her and all I could say is "I don't know". Perhaps if I had told her how Uncle Jim had told me that she wouldn't believe me or how badly hurt she would be, maybe it would have eased the pain. Pain was definitely what my mother was feeling.

Knowing that I had hurt my mother was almost unbearable. I couldn't take it. I begged and pleaded with her not to say anything to anybody about it, but being blessed with the good mother that I had, I should have known that she was not going to let it go without confronting Uncle Jim. It was a confrontation that was far worse than the confrontation that she had with Mrs. Campbell.

Without any hesitation or resistance, my mom just came right out and told my Aunt Dee that I said Uncle Jim had tried to have sex with me. Of course he denied it. He made a lame excuse about me needing attention that I wasn't getting at home, so I just made it all up. He accused me of being mad with him because I wanted him to be my father and he told me no. He pleaded with my Aunt Dee to believe him. He said that I was mixed up with my emotions. He was right about one thing; my emotions were definitely mixed up. I was looking for love, but not in this way.

My poor Aunt Dee was caught in the middle. He was trying to sweet talk her and convince her that I was the one who was lying. With tears streaming down my face, I was trying to persuade her to believe that I would never do anything to hurt her. I pleaded with her to believe that I was telling the truth about Uncle Jim. Emotions were flying high. I wished more than ever that I had never said anything. In fact, I told my mom that I wished that I had never told her and I should have kept it to myself. Uncle Jim yelled at me "Yes you should have kept it to yourself". That is when Aunt Dee knew that what I had said was true. She went into a frenzy. She started hitting him telling him that she wanted him to get out. She was throwing anything that was not nailed down at him screaming at the top of her lungs for him to get out.

In the midst of trying to escape from the claws of Aunt Dee, he whispered to me "This is not over". I did not understand what he meant at the time. But something on the inside made me believe that I would come to find out shortly.

It was not until weeks after the dance that I realized why Uncle Jim took the pictures of me and Mr. Frank and what he meant about he hoped that he didn't have to use them. He had strategized a plan that he hoped would work, but in the event that it didn't he was saving the pictures to use as blackmail to get his revenge against me.

He sent the pictures of me and Mr. Frank to my dad's email. My dad usually checks his email like clockwork, so he knew that my dad would be sure to see the pictures. Sure enough my dad saw the pictures. He was devastated not so much because I went to the Father/ Daughter dance without him but it was because of who I went with. He was appalled that I had gone to the dance with Mr. Frank. He insisted that my mom was in on the plan and was working behind his back. But of course my mom did not know anything about it because I had not told her about it. Convinced that we both were lying and that he could no longer trust anything that either of us said, he decided that he was going to move out.

I pleaded with my dad not to move out. But the more I talked, the faster he seemed to pack his bags. When my dad moved out of the house with me and my mom, it was the worst thing that I could ever imagine. All of his clothes were out of his side of the closet. His dresser drawers were empty. We were mourning, as if we had lost him to a debilitating disease that had caused his death, but he was not dead, just distant in thought, emotion and his will to forgive. He didn't want anything to do with either of us. He was convinced that my mom knew all along that I was talking to Mr. Frank and that she was using me to so she could get back with him. That was not true at all. It was because of my selfishness that our family broke up. If only I had not met Mr. Frank and not gone to the Father/ Daughter Dance. Things could go back to what was normal to us. Life was not perfect, but at least we were all under the same roof. People were talking all over town; some were saying that my mom had put my dad out because she still had feeling for Mr. Frank. There were rumors that my dad had moved out because he had enough of me. That probably was closer to the truth. I know that this was probably the drawing board between me and my dad. Our relationship was doomed forever. I had betrayed my dad. How could I allow another man to take his place? At the time I didn't think about how it would make my dad feel, for another man to take his place.

But to be totally honest, a part of me did not care how he felt. For once he felt some of the pain that I felt on everyday basis practically all my life. He would see how I have felt all of these years, to have a daddy who does not care enough to take part of my life. My friends either didn't know their daddy or their daddy didn't live in the same house with them, but my daddy lived with me and he still didn't take part of my life. That was so embarrassing to me.

For the several months that my dad had moved out and was living with his mother, I tried to keep in contact with him. I would write him letters, but they would all say return to sender. I tried to call and leave him messages, but he would never return my phone calls.

I could see the look in my mom eyes' when she looked at me. I know that she was disappointed in me and my dad. Of all the years that they had been married, they had never been separated. Although many of her family and friends would try to coerce her to leave him, she would always stay. Some of those same family and friends were now telling her to pursue Mr. Frank now that my dad had moved out. But my mom was not that type of woman. She believed in doing the right thing, and she knew that the right thing would not be to date Mr. Frank Simmons.

My mom was committed to my dad, as she had always been. Pursuing another man was definitely not an option for her. She was committed to bridging the gaps and bringing her family back together again. She faithfully prayed and fasted for my dad.

It was subsequent to much praying and fasting, that after almost 8 months, that my father came back home. He didn't give us any prior indication that he was coming home, he just showed up one day bringing in his things and hanging his clothes back on side of the closet. He never did give us a real definitive explanation as to what suddenly made him come back home. He only said that he was back because he wanted to be back.

If I were to ask my mama, she of course would say it was because of the power of God. While I agree with her that God had a lot to do with it, I think that my grandma Lois had something to do it too. Trust me when I say that my dad is not an easy person to live with. He has ways about him that will drive the calm spirited sane person into a panic stricken fit. I figured my father had gotten on my grandma's nerves long enough, that she reached her breaking point, and finally put him out of her house. I guess it really didn't matter why he came back home, that really wasn't important. What was important was he was home in his rightful place. After being separated for 8 months, it was a welcome sight to see my family back together again.

HEADED FOR TROUBLE

Chapter 13

AFTER MY MOM HAD CONFRONTED my uncle about what he had done to me, it seemed that everyone had turned their back on me including my dad. He didn't believe me because I had kept it a secret for so long. In his mind, this was a scheme to get attention. Tina's parents did not want her to talk to me anymore. This was devastating to me. Not only had I been robbed of my innocence, but now I have been robbed of friendship with my best friend. This was pain on a whole new level. It is enough to be victimized by my perpetrator but to be ostracized by the ones who said that they cared about me was enough to send anybody to into a depression.

That is exactly what happened to me. I had suppressed in the back of my mind, the pain of not having my dad's approval, the pain of losing my grandmother and the pain of what my uncle had done to me. I was in such a deep depressed state of mind. I overheard my dad say to my mom that maybe I needed to be locked up in an institution to get some help. It must have been frustrating seeing me walk around in that state of mind, and not knowing what to do to help me. So I guess my dad's solution to the problem was to send me away to an institution. I did not want to go to an institution so I tried my best to fight my depression. But I couldn't hide it from my mom. My mom used to always say that a good mama knows her children and she knows when something isn't right with them. I guess my grandmother was right too when she said "what's in you, will come out". I had so much pain inside of me and it showed. It showed through my attitude and my actions.

All of the things that had happened in my life had begun to change me. I was getting involved in things that under normal circumstances, I would not even be interested in. But I had reached a point in my life that it didn't matter to me what I did, and who I might have hurt in the process. I am sure my mom was hurt by the way that I changed. But the way I saw it was I had already caused her pain by keeping a secret from her, why not just add to the pain.

I didn't care about the same things that I used too. Being successful in school didn't matter to me as much, so my grades were falling behind in school. Although my mom told me that she was there for me and I could always talk to her, I didn't value her opinion as much as I used too. I definitely wasn't the same person that I once was and I certainly wasn't a person that my grandmother would have been proud of. My grandmother had always taught me to be strong and not let situations get the best of me. Deep down inside I was not proud of the person that I had become, but a part of me did not care. Why should I care? Everywhere I was looking for love proved to be a false illusion. I couldn't it find it at home at least not with my dad anyway. I didn't feel loved and accepted at school, and my uncle had betrayed me and I certainly did not feel secure now that my grandmother had died.

My mind deviated from everything that I had been taught. I barricade the lessons about making good choices especially about relationships in the corridor of my mind. My aunts had always taught me that the golden rule to follow was not to date anybody that you wouldn't consider marrying. But I wasn't thinking about getting married. All I was thinking about was having a good time. My grandmother taught me about the importance of having a good reputation. She said that your character says a lot about you and the way that you dress can affect your reputation. She was a firm believer that young ladies were not suppose to show everything that God gave them, but they were suppose to dress appropriately. She said in many cases your good name and your reputation is all that you have so don't ruin. My mom was very adamant about having self respect. She always told me that you can't expect anybody to respect you if you don't respect yourself. She said if you lay down like a doormat, people will walk all over you. Everything that my mother and my grandmother had taught me took a back seat in my mind.

There was only one thing and one thing only that I was focused on and that was developing my relationship with Steven. Steven was 6 ft 2 in slender, muscular, and very handsome quarterback on our football team. I never really thought Steven would be my type. Quite frankly, he was just the type of guy that I had been warned to stay away from. Maybe that is what attracted me to him in the first place.

He was rough and always involved in some mischievous scandal. But he always seemed to escape being punished mainly because he was a star player on the team. There was a lot that came along with being a star player both off and on the field. While on the field, he gained the respect of the other players and coaches because he was aggressive and dominated on the field. Off the field, he was catered too by all of his teachers especially Mr. Waters. Steven knew how to work the system. He had his teachers adhering to his time schedule instead of him abiding by theirs. For example, we had a special project that every student was required to complete and submit to Mr. Waters by the end of the day on 15th of the month. There were no exceptions, it had to be turned in on time or the student would receive a failing grade. Obviously this rule did not apply to Steven because he came to class without his project and Mr. Waters gave him an additional 3 days to get his project complete. He often would come to Mrs. Jay's class complaining about how tired he was, especially if he had played in the game the night before. She would allow him lay his head on his desk and sleep in her class while the rest of us took notes. She would even ask for volunteers for someone to take his notes for Steven. Usually it ended up with Mrs. Jay telling me to take notes for Steven because no one else would volunteer. I guess maybe if Mrs. Jay had offered an incentive for helping Steven out, maybe like a no homework pass, maybe some of the other students would volunteer to do it. It appeared that Steven was getting by and that he had it made but in actuality he wasn't and he didn't have it made. He was only hurting himself by not applying himself and the teachers were only setting him up for failure in the future.

It was my perception that it was inevitable that Steven was doomed for failure and a hard life, but that did not prevent me from wanting to be a part of his clique. I would see him walking and talking with his arms wrapped around the other girls, and I would visualize myself one day being in their place. That day came to fruition one day, when he walked over to me in the lunchroom and with a big smile on his face said "Girl I have been watching you, and you are looking good. I like those jeans you are wearing". I turned around to see who he was talking too. I had to make certain that there was no one else standing behind me. He grabbed my hand, and in a sweet seducing voice, he said "I just want to thank you for taking my notes for me in Mrs. Jay's class. You know I had to get my rest so I can be ready for the game. You helped me out so let me repay you. I am having a party at my house Friday night, why don't you come by". He gave me a piece of paper with his address on it. That was music to my ears. Suddenly it didn't matter that he was allowed to have preferential treatment, while the rest of us worked diligently on completing our tasks on time. I gladly accepted his invitation.

My friend Carl saw Steven talking to me and he wanted to know what he wanted. When I told him that Steven had invited me to a party at his house and that I had accepted, he hit the roof. He was furious that I would even consider associating with a guy like Steven much less going out with him. Everyone knew that Steven had a reputation of being a womanizer. But yet he could still get any girl in the whole school if he wanted her; including me. So for me to be invited to a party at his house was an honor.

Steven had his character flaws, but I was willing to over look them. I overlooked his faults in exchange for his undying love that he had promised to me. Several of my friends, especially Carl told me that Steven wasn't good for me and advised me not to go out with him. But my rationale was that they were all jealous and envious of because I had somebody special in my life and they didn't. I knew that Carl had a crush on me. He is a nice guy who treated me with respect, but I thought of Carl as a brother or a friend of the family. I didn't think of him as the boyfriend type.

To be honest I was confused about what the boyfriend type was. My father had never demonstrated to me how a man is supposed to properly treat a young lady. So the way that Steven acted didn't seem out of the norm for me because that was all that I knew. He was very disrespectful and often said demeaning and rude comments to other young woman.

Refusing to listen to anyone about developing a relationship with Steven, I continued to talk to him. The more I talked to him the more he said the things that I wanted to hear. He had told me that I was the only girl in his life and that he loved me. That was all that I needed to hear. I had built up a trust in him. I believed in him and in everything that he said. He had a way of convincing me to do things that I had never done before.

I knew that my mom would not allow me to go to a party so I told her that I was going over to one of my friend's house. She was ok with that. When I got to the party at Steven's house, he opened the door and said "hey I am glad that you could make it. Come on in and let me introduce you to everyone. He looked at his friends and said "Hey fellas this is my girl Stacey". I greeted all of them with a simple hi, but I was pondering over how Steven had introduced me, as his girl. Did this mean that I was really his girl or was it just the way that he expressed himself?

I saw underage teenagers drinking and smoking, I heard loud obscene music playing. This was not an environment that I was accustomed too. Steven picked up on the fact that I felt uncomfortable. He told me to loosen up and relax and then he handed me an ice cold beer. He said that all the cool kids drunk alcohol and if I wanted to fit in, I needed to drink too. I didn't really want too, but this was my opportunity to fit in with the in crowd. I had seen my dad drink beer before, so I was accustomed to being around beer, but I ask a rhetorical question, "What's this? Misconstruing what I meant by asking what is this, Steven thought I was implying that I wanted something stronger to drink. But before I could explain to him what I meant he said "I like you. I think I could fall in love with a girl like you. That changed everything. Steven hand me a mixed drink and I drank it.

I started coughing and choking; I asked him what's in this? With a sweet innocent voice, he said "Don't worry about it baby. I'll take care of you. Go ahead and take another sip". I told him that I had

had enough. I continued to cough and choke on whatever it was that I was drinking. I didn't know what was mixed in the drink, all I know that it was burning the back of my throat.

Steven took the drink from me and told me to go upstairs with him so we could spend some time alone. Curious as to why we needed to go upstairs, I asked him why we couldn't just stay down stairs. He said "stop asking so many questions, girl. I just want to get to know you better, that's all. I think you can be the only girl for me. I agreed to go upstairs with the exception that we were only going to talk. He promised that that was his only motive.

When we got upstairs we both sat on the bed. He asked me to tell him about myself. I felt like I was on an interview trying to land a job, hoping that I said the right things. He listened attentively as I was talking about the things that had happened in my life. He acted as if he was concerned and offered his condolences about the death of my grandmother and the ordeal that I had gone through with my uncle. We talked for a little while longer, at least until he had grown tired of the small talk. He said I listened to you talk; now why don't you give me a kiss. He caught me by surprised because he had promised that all we were going to do was to talk. But I agreed to give him just one kiss. We kissed for about a minute. Steven looked deep in my eyes and said "see now that wasn't so bad was it"? He pressed his lips against mine and started to try to unbutton my shirt. I grabbed his hand and told him to stop. But he kept trying to grab the buttons on my shirt. I kept yelling, stop what are you doing, but he wouldn't.

By that time Steven's friends enter the room. They all started pulling on me trying to take my clothes off. I was kicking and screaming STOP! STOP! STOP! Steven in turn would say come on you know you like it. You liked it with your uncle didn't you? I was screaming and crying, "Please let me go". Steven and his friends all kept ripping my clothes off, and by this time, Steven was furious because I wouldn't cooperate. He kept saying "Come on girl stop acting like you don't like it".

In a sudden impulse, I grabbed and mercilessly bit a chunk out of Steven's ear. For the first time in this whole ordeal, he was now the one who was screaming. He jumped up holding his ear, with blood dripping down the side of his neck, he yelled "ouch! What's the matter with you girl? Why did you bite me"? You are crazy girl. I looked at him with a look of sweet revenge in my eyes and I said "You let me go now!!!! Steven looked at his friends and told them "let her go, she isn't worth it".

With most of my clothes ripped from my body, I held on to what was remaining, and ran out of Steven's house. As I was walking down the street out of the clear blue sky Carl drove up in his green Volkswagen. He stopped and pulled his car over, got out and wrapped his coat around me and told me to get in. I tried to explain to him what had happened, but all I could get out was "Carl . . . . they tried to . . . . then I pushed them off . . . . I screamed . . . . I was scared. Carl was furious. With a puzzled look on his face, he said "They? Who is they? Tell me who did this to you? What are their names? I will get them. He then proceeded to turn his car around headed back in the direction of the party. Panicky, I screamed for him not to go back. He continued to race his car full speed like a participant in the Daytona 500 lap race. I pleaded with him to slow down so that we wouldn't get hurt. I was afraid that we were going to flip over in the car, that's how fast Carl was going. I feared for our lives. "Slow down Carl, please just slow down". Finally Carl came to his senses and stopped the car. He grasped the steering wheel of the car and just banged his head on it. I could feel that he was filled with mixed emotions. A part of him was hurt that this had happened, but another part of him was angry because I did not listen. If I had taken his advice and listened in the first place, none of this would have happened.

I apologized to him. He grabbed me and pulled me close to him and said "its okay, Stacey! You are safe now! That's all that matters! I will take care of you.

Carl started back driving. There was a piercing silence for a brief moment. Then finally Stacey broke the silence and asked "you are never on this side of town, where were you doing over here tonight"? I just had a gut instinct that you were in some kind of trouble and you were going to need me.

Carl had been saved for a while and he had learned about the Holy Ghost. He knew that it was the Holy Ghost that had lead him to go and get Stacey. I asked him, "Well aren't you going to say I told you so"? Looking straight ahead, he said "No I'm not! There is no need too. But I do hope that you will listen to me next time". With so much remorse, I said I wish I had listened to you. You were trying to warn me and I didn't listen. I know it's all my fault. Being the kind, sweet and understanding guy that Carl was, he reassured me that it was not my fault and that they should not have done what they did to me. I was glad that Carl felt that way, but a part of me knew that it was only right that I take ownership for my part in what had happened. It might not have been my fault for what they had done to me, but I had committed some acts of sin as well, like lying to my mom about where I really was, going to an unsupervised party where there smoking and drinking, going upstairs to a bedroom with a boy. What was I thinking? I should have known better, but why didn't it? Was I that desperate for someone to love me that I would subject myself to that kind of humiliation? I was angry with myself. How could I ever look at myself in the mirror without seeing the utter disgust glaring back at me.

As Carl dropped me off at home, I thanked him for all that he had done to help me. Just as any good friend would do, he gave me the assurance that I had his full support. I sure did need his support, because I honestly thought that this would get the best of me.

As time went on thoughts of suicide started to enter my mind. Life had dealt me a bad hand, and I didn't know how to cope anymore. I felt that I didn't have anything else to live for. I just couldn't handle life anymore. Listening to my dad over the years rant and rave about me was enough to push me over the edge, and I had managed to survive, but now having to deal with this situation was more than I could handle. In my mind suicide was my only option. I thought all of the different ways that I could end my life. I had planned to take an overdose of pills. I went to the bathroom rumbling through the medical cabinet. I knew that my dad had some pills in there that I could take. I searched until I found the sleeping pills that Dr. Steven had prescribed my dad. When I found them I went to my bedroom and wrote a suicide note to my mom. I wrote these words: Mom, I am so sorry, but I just couldn't take it anymore. I will always love you. Now I won't have to worry about being hurt anymore. This is what is best. Tell daddy he got his wish and now he doesn't have to worry about loving me anymore. I took a handful of pills and that is the last thing that I remember, but apparently I passed out. If it had not been for Carl my mom might not have found me until the next morning. But Carl had another gut instinct and he came over. My mom and dad were sitting in the living room watching television, and there was a knock at the door. My mother answered the door. It was Carl. Before she could say anything, Carl said "hello Mrs. Alexander I know that it is late, but I was wondering if I could talk with Stacey. My mom replied "Yes it is late Carl and you know that I don't usually allow Stacey to have company past a certain time. But I will let you talk to her this time, but next time you come here earlier, don't come to my house this late anymore. Wait right here". She walked to the edge of the stair case and she called my name "Stacey! Stacey! Stacey! You have company! Carl is here Stacey!

My mom thought that I must have had my headphones on listening to music, so she walked upstairs headed to my room. She was still calling my name, as she walked into my room. Much to her surprise, she found me lying on the floor. She screamed to the top of her lungs "Oh my God, come here Michael". Both my dad and Carl ran upstairs. Carl was the first one to find the note that I had left. My mom kept screaming telling my dad to call 911. But my dad just stood in the doorway staring at me. Maybe he was in shock or maybe he just didn't care. Finally Carl got the phone and called 911 and handed the phone to my mom. My mom talked to the dispatcher:

911 OPERATOR
911 What is your emergency?
REBECCA
My daughter is hurt

911 OPERATOR
How is she hurt ma'am?

REBECCA
(screaming hysterically)
I found her laying on the floor and an empty bottle of pills.

911 OPERATOR
I need you to calm down ma'am. Now what is your name?

REBECCA
My name is Rebecca Alexander. Hurry; send
somebody to help my daughter.

911 OPERATOR
Mrs. Alexander, calm down, now what is your address?

REBECCA
912 Elm Place, Hurry please!

911 OPERATOR
I am dispatching a paramedic now. I want you to
stay on the line until someone gets there.

911 OPERATOR
Mrs. Alexander is your daughter breathing?

REBECCA
I don't know.

911 OPERATOR
I need you to put your hand over her mouth and
nose to check to see if she is breathing.

REBECCA
No! No! She is not breathing. I don't feel a pulse.

By that time the ambulance arrived at our house to take me to the
hospital. My mom grabbed her coat, her purse and the bottle of
pills that I had taken. She was headed out the door when she looked
and saw that my dad was just standing there. She said "Michael the
ambulance is here, come on let's go. He refused to go to the hospital
with my mom. For the first time, Carl stood up to my dad. He said
to him, "with all due respect, I think that you should go. Stacey

needs you". What kind of father would not go to the hospital with his daughter? My dad cleared his throat and said "she doesn't need me. She has her mama. Her mama can handle it.

Carl rode in the ambulance with me holding my hand. He was crying and pleading with me "Don't you do this to me! You can pull through this! Stacey you can get through this! Fight! Fight hard! God please help her!

We arrived at the hospital. Lying there still and lifeless, the paramedics rushed to get me out of the ambulance and into the hospital. Dr. Steven was the doctor on call that night. The paramedics informed him of the type of pills that I had taken. Dr. Steven and his team immediately began working on me trying to save me before it was too late. They washed my stomach out by gastric lavage or stomach pumping to mechanically remove the unabsorbed drugs from my stomach. I was given charcoal to help bind the drugs in my stomach and intestines, so it would be a less amount absorbed in my blood.

I was in bad shape, but I pulled through. I am convinced that it was the grace of God and the prayers that were prayed. Dr. Steven came to talk to my mom. He said "Mrs. Alexander we worked with your daughter, she will be alright. She was truly blessed. I just wanted you to know that I will be writing an order for her to have a psychological evaluation. I do think that she needs to have a psychological evaluation done.

If you don't mind I would like to ask you a few questions, Dr. Steven said to my mom. Do you have any idea what would make your daughter do something like this"? Without any hesitation, my mom blurted out "no! No I don't!" Dr. Steven was not convinced that my mom did not have any idea, so he kept prying her for more information. You haven't noticed any changes in her behavior lately? This time my mom admitted that I had a few challenges, but she didn't realize that it bothered me. He dung a little deeper and asked my mom "how is your relationship with your daughter and why didn't she come to you with her problems"? My mom took offense with the question that he posed to her. She said "I don't know what you are getting at, but my daughter and I have a good relationship". He popped the big question, "What about with your husband, her dad? My mom hesitated briefly and she said "they have some issues but he loves her in his own way". That was always the excuse that my mom used when it came to her talking about my daddy's love for me. It was an excuse that Dr. Steven recognized as an excuse and told my mom he did. He gave her a message that she probably didn't want to hear, but needed to hear. He said to her "Mrs. Alexander it seems that you are making excuses for your husband. You can't make excuses for his behavior. If you do you are just as guilty as he is". Needless to say, my mom was highly offended, she did not feel as though that neither she nor my dad was the blame for what I had done.

Dr. Steven did not agree at all. He said my mom might not be all of the reason that I had tried to end my life, but she was certainly a part of the reason. He was convinced that I was in pain and was crying out for help. He said in order for me to get better, he would strongly recommend family counseling. The first response out of my mom's mouth was "my husband will never agree to that". She was right too. My dad would never agree to go to counseling session because he thought it was a waste of his time. But little did he know, that the Bay Chip counseling center offered a service that allowed the counselor to make home visits. So that is what we did. My mom signed a form indicating that she wanted a counselor to come to our house and talk with our family.

On the first day that Mrs. Jones was scheduled to come to our house for the first session, my dad was at work. This gave Mrs. Jones time to talk to me and my mom, but mostly me. She asked me simple questions in the beginning, I guess so she could break the ice, and make everyone feel comfortable. But then she asked me some tough questions, like why did I try to hurt myself? I told her that my whole life changed when my Grandma Mattie died. My uncle Jim betrayed me. He said that he would do all the things for me that my dad never did. Then I found out that this boy who I thought liked me was only using me. He didn't love me.

Mrs. Jones listened and sympathized with me as if she knew exactly how I felt. She nodded her head as to say keep going. So I did. I told her that I really didn't want to hurt myself. I just had so much pain that I didn't know what to do with. She was sure to point out to me that trying to commit suicide is never the answer. I knew that she was right. I kept talking. I said "you know the worst part about everything that I was going through was"? Mrs. Jones said that she didn't know, so I told her. I went through all of this and my daddy act like he didn't even care. My daddy doesn't love me. He never has. I guess in my mind if he would have said that everything would have been alright, and then I would have been alright. Maybe I could have handle things better, if he was there. But he wasn't.

She acted shocked over what I had said, but I got a feeling that she really wasn't shocked. She asked me what makes you think that your daddy doesn't love you"? I replied "he never told me".

Mrs. Jones reiterated what I had said "you are 15 years old and you have never heard your daddy tell you that he loves you". Mrs. Jones looked at my mom and asked her if she heard what I had just said. Surely she had to know that my mom heard me since she was sitting in the room with us, but I think she asked my mom that question because she really wanted it to sink in. Mrs. Jones turned her attention back to me, "Stacey is this where all of your problems stem from, your daddy not loving you. I told her "I don't know. I mean I guess so. I think sometime maybe if I had my daddy's love, I would not have been looking for love. Maybe I would not have made so many stupid mistakes.

Just then we heard the key rattling in the door. It was my dad. My mom excused herself and went to greet my dad. They both walked back to the living room where Mrs. Jones and I were sitting. Mrs. Jones stood up and held out her hand, while shaking my dad's hand she said "Hello, Michael, may I call you Michael? I'm Christie Jones from the Bay Chip Center". In his sarcastic way, he said "May I call you Christie? Why are you here? Wait a minute that's that place for crazy folk isn't it? Mrs. Jones apologetically said to my dad "I know that you are just getting home, but if I can I would like to take a few moments of your time. I want to talk to you about your daughter Stacey". My dad paraded around the room like he had found a lost treasure, I knew it! I've been saying it all along. I knew something was wrong with her. I finally got somebody on my side to prove what I have been saying all along. Yes, I will sit down! Gladly! So you can prove that she is crazy". It was from this point that the whole dynamics of the conversation changed.

COUNSELOR

Mr. Alexander this is not why I am here. But it's interesting
to me why you would call your daughter crazy.

MICHAEL

I call her crazy because she is crazy. She is always in her room
cooped up like she is a hermit. She is not smart. She is always
falling behind. She is not outgoing at all. Do I need to go on?

COUNSELOR

Have you ever checked to see what she is doing in her room?
Have you ever asked her why she spends so much time in her
room? Do you ever volunteer to help her with her homework?

MICHAEL

Hey this is not about me.

COUNSELOR

You are absolutely right. You have a beautiful
daughter, Mr. Alexander. Do you have any idea why
your daughter would try to hurt herself?

MICHAEL

Nope! Crazy I guess!

COUNSELOR

Mr. Alexander, it is a cry out for help. Your daughter needs your
attention. She is longing for your love and acceptance of her.
She needs you to be for the good times and the bad times.

COUNSELOR

Did you know that Stacey has so much pain in her heart and
she just didn't know how to handle what she was feeling?

COUNSELOR

Do you know where all this pain is coming from?

MICHAEL

Nope

COUNSELOR

It came from you being an emotional absent father.

MICHAEL
You wait one minute you are not going to come
in my house and attack me like this.

COUNSELOR
I am not attacking you. But let's keep it real some of the
things that's she does is a direct reflection of the way you
have treated her. Your daughter was willing to end her
life because of you. How does that make you feel?

Michael jumps out of his seat and starts walking out.

MICHAEL
She's the problem not me. As far as I am
concerned she could have died.

WORDS OF WISDOM

Chapter 14

W HAT HAPPENED TO ME WAS the talk all over the school. Every hall and every classroom seemed to have someone engaged in a conversation about what happened. Mrs. Bertha, an old woman who must have been in her 60's, works as our school librarian. She said, "Come here baby let me talk to you. I ain't trying to make you feel no worse than you already do, but you brought this on yourself. You were taught better. I bet your grand mama is just turning over in her grave. Now you don't need nobody to validate you, but especially don't need no boy like you was out with the other night. You are too smart for that. Keep yourself up and have respect for yourself. Don't be with nobody that don't mean you any good. Remember if you lay down with dogs, you will get up with fleas.

And what's this about you taking pills trying to hurt yourself? Baby, I know that you have been through a lot and you might be hurting, but there is nothing so bad that you need to try to end your life. Life is precious honey; it's a gift from God. You have to treasure it. Don't let nothing or nobody get next to you like that. You hear me! I imagine that you miss your Grandma Mattie, don't you?

I told her "Yes ma'am I do. I miss her so much! She said I know you do. She's gone now, but I am here for you. I can't take her place, can't anybody fill her shoes, but I will do my best to help you. I want you to ask your mama if it will be alright for you to come by house sometime. Just tell her I need you to keep me company.

What Ms. Bertha said made a whole lot of sense. I was so glad that she talked to me. It is amazing how Ms. Bertha knows everything. In her own way she looks out for us. Sometimes we did things that we were not supposed to. I honestly believe that it was Ms. Bertha who told on us. She kept us straight. She used to say, your parents didn't send you out to this school to be a class clown. They want you to get an education.

Ms. Bertha was a good ole fashioned church going woman. She was convinced that half of the kid's problems at school were that we didn't go to church and parents are not doing their jobs. She said parents are not the same as they used to be. Parents today let their children tell them what to do. They try to be the child friend instead of the parent. Not me, I didn't let my son boss me around. God bless his soul'.

I used to wonder about how Ms, Bertha knew so much about kids when she didn't have any kids of her own. Well she had a son, but he was killed. I couldn't imagine how she felt to have only one son, and he was killed. My mama didn't say much about his death, just that it was an accident. I have not heard Ms. Bertha say much about her son. But she sure does have a lot of pictures of him in her living room. I know she must have loved him and miss him so much. I wondered how Ms. Bertha could be so nice and caring to people when she has so much pain. Her husband, Mr. Thomas James Wilson, TJ for short, had died of a massive heart attack two years after their son had died. A lot of people say that their son's death was the reason that her husband died. That was what was said about her husband's death, but what about her son. How did he die? I sure did want to know. I figured the only way that I was going to ever know what happened to him was to ask. So that is just what I planned to do. But, how would I ask her? When would be the perfect time to talk about something so personal? I tried to figure out the perfect time to ask her. Finally, I just made up my mind to come right out and ask her.

My mom asked me to go to Ms. Bertha's house to give her the cake pans that she wanted to borrow. So I figured that this would be a good time to talk to Ms. Bertha about her son. I got to her house and as usual my eye caught the array of all the pictures of her son. I saw one picture of her son sitting on the mantle over the fireplace.

The picture was in a picture frame with basketball around the corners. The boy in the picture appeared to be around 16 years old. He was dressed in a light blue cap with TJ written in white letters. He had a light blue jersey to match his cap. What really stood out to me was his big smile that seemed to go from ear to ear. Just by looking at the picture it seemed to tell a story. Looking at the picture he seemed to be happy, but I later found out that was further from the truth.

I decided to go ahead and ask Ms. Bertha about the picture. I cleared my throat but only was able to speak above a mere whisper because I was so scared. But I knew that I had to ask her. With my hands shaking nervously like a leaf on a tree, I picked up the picture of her son, and I called her name, "Ms. Bertha". She said "What is it child"? I asked her "Who is this?" Then there was quietness that seemed eerie. Ms. Bertha stared at me with an empty look. The expression on her face was like a blank sheet of paper waiting to be written on. It took a few minutes, but finally Ms. Bertha said "That's my baby boy". I knew that already, but I really wanted to know was what happened to him. So I asked her. Where is he? I mean what happened to him. She told me to sit down and she began to tell me the story about her son. She started off by telling me that he was a good boy. He was smart and did really good in school. He loved helping out at the church. He always had good manners. That's the way we raised him. I did not have a bit of trouble out of him. The most thing that I ever had to worry about was him not keeping his room clean. That is until he started hanging around those boys that lived on the other side of town. I knew they were trouble from the start. They thought that they were fooling me, giving me a slick smile, and always saying yes ma'am. But they were not fooling me, I could see right through them".

All the trouble started when Jr. would come late from school. He said that he was going to the park to play ball. But something in my spirit told me that it was more to it than that. So like any good mother would do, I asked him about it and I told him that I didn't want him to hang with those boys anymore because they were trouble.

Now child you have to understand. I tried to talk to those boys before. I tried to help them in any way that I could. I told them about

Jesus and how they needed to get to know him for themselves. I even invited them to go to church with me. But they just laughed in my face. So now honey I just pray for them. I pray that God will touch their hearts before it is too late.

Ms. Bertha began to cry as she began to tell me exactly how her son died. Sobbing helplessly, she said "They didn't have to do what they did to my baby. They set my baby up! They set my baby up! He didn't know any better. He just wanted to fit in. They took my baby down to that store and they dared him to steal something. It didn't matter what he stole—just as long as he stole something. He picked up a candy bar and put it in his pocket. As soon as he did, they told Mr. W.J. Smith. He was the owner of the store. My boy didn't know what was going on until he saw the look on Mr. W. J. Smith's face. My baby got scared and he tried to run, but he didn't run fast enough. Mr. W. J. Smith was angry with all the boys; he was so angry that he got his gun and started shooting. He shot my baby. Mr. W.J. Smith is a free man, but my baby is 6 ft under. Every day I have to look in the face of Mr. W.J. Smith and those boys who did this to my baby and they just turn their heads. They ain't never ever said I'm sorry or anything. But I forgive them.

I asked Ms. Bertha how could she forgive them for what they did? She told me "This thing called love". That's when she told me about God's love and his forgiveness. She told me that God wants us to forgive people no matter what they do. He forgives us for the sins that we commit. She said that it said in the Bible that we don't forgive others than God would not forgive us.

Everyday I would go to Ms. Bertha's house and listen to her tell me something about the Bible. I would go back home and tell my mom and my dad what I learned from Ms. Bertha. My mom was excited about what I was learning. But my dad, on the other hand, did not pay any attention to me. He would tell me that he didn't want to hear anything about that Jesus stuff. But something on the inside of me kept pressuring me to keep telling him about what Ms. Bertha said about Jesus. So I did. Every day when I came back home from Ms. Bertha's house, I would sit in the living room and tell my dad what I learned from Ms. Bertha. Everyday my dad would yell at me and say mean things to me. I guess he thought if he could say something to hurt my feelings, maybe I would stop telling him about Jesus. But to be honest, the more I talked to him about Jesus, the less his yelling seemed to bother me. I kept praying for my dad and asking God to save him.

One thing I knew for sure about Ms. Bertha was that she loved to talk about Jesus. I think that she looked forward to our special Jesus and Me" tea just as much as I did. I called them Jesus and Me tea because we always drunk tea when Ms. Bertha taught me about Jesus.

Ms. Bertha also loved going to church and would invite anyone who wanted to come. One Sunday, she invited my family and me to go to church with her. They were having a Family and Friends Day celebration. My mom and I went, but my dad did not go. Mrs. Bertha saw us as we walked in the church. She had a surprised look on her face as if she was looking for someone else to come along with us. To ease her mind and her curiosity, I told her that only my mom had come and not my dad. In a very confident manner, she looked at me and simply replied "he will be here soon enough". I knew that she was in touch with God, so I couldn't help but wonder if God had revealed something to her. Ms. Bertha, my mom and I sat together listening attentively as Rev. Smith preached his sermon.

As he was preaching I had a conversation with God. Now God I am coming to you. I want to feel your love. I have been looking and searching for your love. Let me feel your love. I want to know what real love is.

It was as if he was talking to me when he said "There is somebody here who has been looking for love in all the wrong places". You who have come that might have pain, and be in misery, you are in the right place. I want you to know that true love in found in a relationship with Jesus. The Bible says in John 3:16 "For God so loveth the world that he gave his only begotten son, that whosoever shall believe in his heart shall not perish but have everlasting life". He said that God died for us all that and he loved us all the same. It didn't matter how many mistakes that you might have made in your life that God will forgive you because he loves you.

After he preached, he extended the invitation to the congregation for prayer and to accept Jesus as our savior. Several people walk to the altar including me. I told Rev. Smith that I wanted to be saved.

I want my life to be different. I wanted to feel loved. He told each of us who had come to the altar to close our eyes and repeat after him. I repeated after him "Lord I confess that I am a sinner, I ask that you come into my heart and forgive me of my sins. I believe that your son Jesus died on the cross, stayed in the grave for three days and rose again. I accept Jesus as my Lord and Savior. Then Rev. Smith said If you were sincere about the prayer that you just prayed you are now a born again believer. Welcome to the family.

I don't think I will ever be able to put into words of how I felt that day. It was as if a heavy burden was lifted off of me. I was not angry with my father anymore. I didn't carry unforgiveness around anymore. For the first time in my life, I felt free. I felt a peace that I cannot explain. It was a peace that I knew only God could give.

I was so excited. Even more excited than going to the Father/Daughter dance with Mr. Frank. I can remember going home to tell my dad about me getting saved. I race through the house jumping up and down shouting "Daddy! Daddy! He came out of the kitchen, and asked "what's the matter with me, and why was I calling his name so loudly. In a jovial way, I said, "Guess what? His response was "I don't have time to play any guessing games, if you are going to tell me something, go ahead and tell me". I did gladly. I shouted "I got saved today". My dad laughed and "Oh no, now you are going to be acting spooky too. You will be acting spooky just like your mama does. She always wants to pray about everything. Sometimes when she prays she sounds like she is speaking jibber jabber. Then he started pretending that he was speaking in tongues. I didn't know everything there was to know about God, but I did have sense enough to know that it was not good to play with God. "See you sound just like your mama, always taking things too serious", was his response. He didn't think that it was serious, but it was. Both Ms. Bertha and Rev. Smith had said that accepting Jesus was the best decision that I could have ever made.

I was glad that I had made my decision to accept Jesus as my Savior. I made sure that my dad knew that I was glad too. Before I could go any further in sharing my good news, my dad stopped me in my tracks and made it perfectly clear that he was not interested in getting saved. He didn't need Jesus in his life and there was nothing that I could say or do to change his mind. He said my mom had been trying for years and she couldn't make him change.

I continued going to Ms. Bertha's house for our Jesus and me teas, but I started reading the Bible on my own. I started reading scriptures like 1 Peter 2:9 "But you are a chosen generation, a royal priesthood, a holy nation, a people for his own; that you should show forth the praises of him who has called you out of darkness into his marvelous light". Romans 8:37 "Nay, in all these things we are more than conquerors through him that loved us. Philippians 4:13 "I can do all things through Christ which strengthened me". Jeremiah 29:11" For I know the plans I have for you," declares the LORD, "plans to prosper you and not to harm you, plans to give you hope and a future". Ephesians 3:20 "Now unto him who is able to do exceeding abundantly above all that we can ask or think". I read these and so many more scriptures. The more I read the more empowered I felt and the stronger I became. The stronger I grew in my relationship with God, the more I realized that I had been wrong about Him. I used to think that God was just like my daddy, but I was wrong. With God he accepted me just the way I was, and I didn't have to work hard to earn His love. In fact I didn't have to work for love at all; it came automatic with no strings attached.

I kept inviting my dad to come to church. Each time he would make an excuse as to why he couldn't go. Although he wouldn't admit it, I know that he could see the change that had taken place in my life. There was still a lot that I had to learn, but I had experience enough in my life to be able to tell my father the difference Jesus had made in my life. I was faithful in telling my dad about what I had learned from Ms. Bertha and going to church. Of course, my father continued to play hard, saying that he didn't need to hear what I had to say. I pleaded with him to go to church with me. I was desperate for him to feel the way I felt about Jesus. I was so passionate about my dad's salvation, that I prayed a special prayer that God would use me to lead my dad to his Son Jesus so that he could receive salvation.

GOD'S SPECIAL PLAN

Chapter 15

O VER THE COURSE OF A couple of months my dad started back having reoccurring headaches. My mom said that my dad used to always complain about having headaches, but He insisted on that the doctors were not really concerned about his health and only wanted his money, so he would not go to the doctor. Time passed by, and without any explanation, the headaches went away. A whole year went by and he did not have a single headache; until now. Now not only is he experiencing excruciating pain in the center and the back of his head, he is also started having episodes of where he would feel faint and dizzy and he had frequent urination. My dad had associated frequent urination with the excessive amount of beer that he drank on a regular basis.

Worried that the symptoms that he was having, was sure indication that his blood pressure was elevated, my mom tried to convince my dad to go to the doctor. He kept resisting. This went on for a period of time. The more my mom and others tried to convince him to go the doctor, the more he resisted. It was only after that he started having problems with his vision being blurry, that he decided to go to the doctor. It was his assumption that maybe he had some type of infection and that Dr. Richardson would give him antibiotics and send him home. That was not what happened. Alarmed by the blood in my dad's urine, Dr. Richardson decided that a biopsy needed to be performed to help form a diagnosis and choose the best course of treatment. Upon Dr. Richardson examining my father, the tests and biopsy revealed that my father's kidneys were not functioning properly. Over the course of years that my dad had had problems with his headaches which were a result of his elevated blood pressure, his kidneys were affected.

Dr. Richardson tried to explain to my dad about how high blood pressure can affect a person's body. He told him high blood pressure makes the heart work harder and, over time, can damage blood vessels throughout the body. If the blood vessels in the kidneys are damaged, they may stop removing wastes and extra fluid from the body. The extra fluid in the blood vessels may then raise blood pressure even more. It's a dangerous cycle. My dad was not really interested in hearing what Dr. Richardson had to say, all he wanted to know where what was the next course of action. How was this problem going to be solved?

Dr. Richardson told my dad that he had waited too late to get the help that he needed and that in his medical opinion, he would recommend that he start on dialysis.

Dialysis is a treatment which mechanically filters waste that builds up in the bloodstream when the kidneys cease to function. He explained that being on dialysis was very time consuming and labor intensive. He would have to go to a dialysis center at least 3 times a week to have his blood cleansed. It was hard to embrace the fact that he was not well, but now to hear that he would have to be on dialysis was too much for him. My dad did not want to give up so much of his freedom, and not be able to live an active lifestyle that he was accustomed. Dr. Richardson enlightened my dad about the only other options and that was to have a kidney transplant. He explained about the pros and cons about having a kidney transplant. He told him that in order to be a good candidate for a transplant, he would have to make sure that my dad was healthy enough to undergo major surgery and to tolerate a strict, lifelong medication regimen after surgery. With strong emphasis, he told my dad "You must also be willing and able to follow all of my instructions and take your medications regularly. Are you willing to do that Michael?

With a sigh and a slight ray of hope, my dad exclaimed, "yes, yes I am willing to do whatever it takes".

If you are indeed willing to do whatever it takes, you will need to be evaluated at a transplant center. This evaluation usually requires that you make several visits to assess your physical, psychological, and familial condition. The doctors will run tests on your blood and urine and give you a complete physical exam to ensure you're healthy enough for surgery.

A psychologist and a social worker will also meet with you to make sure you are able to understand and follow a complicated treatment regimen. The social worker will make sure you can afford the procedure and that you have adequate support after you are released from the hospital.

If you are approved for a transplant, either a family member can donate a kidney, or you will be placed on a waiting list. Let me warn you that this is not an easy process.

My dad left the doctor's office and came home to tell my mom what Dr. Richardson had said. It was apparent that he was upset about something as soon as he walked in the front door. My mom went to the door to greet him just as she always does, he walked right past her. This was unusual, even for my dad. He sat on the edge of the bed with his head in his hands with a sad look on his face. My mom asked "what's wrong Michael. He began to tell my mom what Dr. Richardson had said; "Dr. Richardson said something about how high blood pressure makes a person's heart work harder and, over time, it can damage blood vessels throughout the body. Then if the blood vessels in the kidneys are damaged, they may stop removing wastes and extra fluid from the body. The extra fluid in the blood vessels is what causes the blood pressure even more. He said that is dangerous. He looked at my mom and told her that he wished he had listened to her and gone to the doctor sooner.

I could not believe my ears. My dad was actually admitting that my mom had been right about something and he was wrong for not listening. He actually apologized to my mom. To my recollection I had never heard my dad apologize to anyone especially my mom. This really led me to believe that he was afraid. Another reason I think that he was full of fear, was he was receptive to the idea of praying. In fact, it was his idea to pray. For the first time, he reached out to my mom for prayer. He wanted my mom to pray because he was certain that God would not hear his prayer. My mom prayed "Lord we come to you thanking you for your goodness. Lord this situation that we are in seems hard, but we know that there is nothing too hard for you. God the doctors say that Michael needs a kidney transplant. We ask you to work a miracle and heal Michael. God you are a healer! We are depending on you to God, Jehovah Rapha and we say that it is done in your son Jesus' name. Amen. The Holy Spirit was upon my mom and she started speaking in tongues. I have seen times that my dad would be laughing at my mom picking at her, saying that she is speaking jibber jabber. But he was not laughing this time. This was not a laughing matter.

As my mom and dad prayed, I prayed along with them asking God for a miracle for my dad. Shortly after my prayer, I felt a strong wave of peace and I knew immediately that I wanted to help my dad. I told my mom that I wanted to give my dad one of my kidneys. My mom drilled me with question to make certain if that was what I really wanted to do. It really didn't boil down too if I wanted to do it, but it was without question something that I knew that I had to do. It was a matter of life or death for my dad, so I knew that I had to step up and do what was right. My mom told my dad that I was willing to give him one of my kidneys. Both my mom and I thought that he would be overjoyed, but to our surprise he was not. Although he was facing a life or death situation, his first response was that he didn't want a part of me inside of him. Those words hurt me, but I did not let that stop my decision. I had already made up my mind to help him and that was what I had intended to do. One thing that I had learned from Ms. Betsy was I am not responsible for the way other people treat me, but I am responsible for the way that I treat other people. Just because my dad did not show love to me was not a reason for me not to show love to him.

Although my dad had left open wounds in my life, I was so proud of myself that I had reached a point where I was able to look past the hurt and pain and help him in his time of need. I am certain that what Ms. Betsy had taught me during our Jesus and me teas had a big influence on the decision that I had made. It was also because of my relationship with God that I had grown stronger. I wasn't the weak kid who was in search of a father's love, but because of God's strength I was a strong kid whose mission was centered on helping my dad find God's love. I knew that if my dad had God's love then I could have my dad's love. The way that I saw it; it was a win /win situation. In the back of my mind, I couldn't help but wonder was God going to use this situation to draw my dad to salvation. Was all of this a part of his plan?

I went to the doctor's office to be tested to see if I was a match for a donor for my dad's kidney transplant. As it turns out, I was a match. The next day both my father and I were admitted into the hospital. We were both given an IV. A surgeon came in to see if we had any more questions. We signed a consent form and then we were wheeled back to the operating room. The anesthesiologist gave us medicine to help us relax. Four hours later we were in the recovery room. Although he was groggy from the medication, for the first time my dad gave me a look of approval and said, "We made it through". With a smile from ear to ear, I said "yes we did".

Without any inclination that Nurse Judy would be one of the nurses to take care of us, she came to my dad's bed and said, "Hello, Mr. Alexander, I just wanted to come by to check on the two of you. See I told you the day she was born that she was extra special and she would do something great." She walked off with a big smile on her face.

After a week or so, we were dismissed from the hospital. My dad was home recuperating. It was as I taking my dad's dirty dishes back to the kitchen, that he finally asked me, "Tell me something. Why did you volunteer to help me? You didn't have to do it."

I gazed into my dad's eyes and said "I Know that I didn't have too, but it was love that made me want too. He did not have a clue about what I was talking about. So I explained to him as best I could. I told him it was because of what Ms. Bertha had taught me about forgiveness that I was able to forgive him. This turned the conversation into a whole other level.

He could not possibly understand what I had to forgive him for. He had not done anything, at least in his mind he hadn't.

I didn't want to get into a confrontation with my dad, but I knew that I had to take this opportunity to tell him the feelings that I had grown up with. I looked in my dad's eyes and I told him "you were not there for me". Now we undoubtedly had a different impression on what not being there for me meant. He felt that because he was in the house with me, he kept a roof over my head, he provided food for me to eat and clothes to wear that that was all to it to being a father. But in my mind, it was much more to it than that. I needed a father who was there emotionally. I gave him his due respect for being there physically, but I needed him to be there emotionally. I told him "Daddy all of my life I have wanted to hear you say that I love you. I tried my best to do things that would make you love me". I told him every little girl wants to be loved by her father. I needed his love more than his money. I needed him to take the time to show me how I was supposed to be treated by a young man. I honestly didn't know because he had not set a good example when it came to how he treated me and my mother. He didn't seem to understand that the way that a father treats his daughter is what she will look for in a guy that she dates. That was exactly what I did. That was the reason I dated Steven. He treated me the way I was used to be treated. I was used to my daddy and yelling at me and putting me down. That is what Steven did and I accepted it.

I felt a sense of relief after I talked with my dad although he didn't seem to understand what I was telling him. I felt that a burden had been lifted off of me and I was relieved that I had a chance to talk to him.

For the next couple of Sundays, I invited my dad to come to church with me. Each Sunday he would decline and try to pacify me by telling me that he would go the next Sunday. But he never would go. I thought surely after the ordeal with his kidneys that he would be more than eager to go to church. I was for certain that he would have a hunger to learn more about God. I knew beyond the shadow of a doubt that he would want to give God praise for bringing him through. But he did not appear thankful at all. The more I talked to him about God sparing his life; he took as me trying to rub it in his face that I gave him one of my kidneys. He would say that he knew he got lucky. But luck had nothing to do with it. It was because of God's grace and love that my dad's life was spared.

I was not trying to rub anything in my dad's face. That was not the case at all. I really wanted my dad to go to church. I wanted him to have a desire to go on his own and not because I asked him to go. He would tell me that he would go when he got ready. I tried to explain to him that the enemy would never let him get ready because he doesn't want him to go to church. He of course did not want to hear anything about the enemy and his power. As far as my dad was concerned he was in full control and nothing or nobody could stop him from doing what he wanted to do.

My dad was physically well, but he was still spiritually sick. When a person is physically sick, they go the hospital, well the church is the hospital for people who are spiritually sick. I knew that if my dad went to church he would hear something that would change his life.

My mom and I left home and went to church. My dad stayed at home as usual. Usually my dad would stay in bed and sleep or if he decided to get up, he would read the newspaper or a sports magazine. But there was one particular Sunday that I will never forget. This time it was different, instead of doing any of those things, this time he felt led to watch television. He turned the television on, and he was flipping through the channels. It seemed that every channel that he saw had someone preaching. One preacher was preaching about God's love and gift of salvation. Not knowing at the time that my dad was watching the television broadcast, I was praying to God that he would touch his heart.

Rev. Smith continued to preach about God's love. As always, after preaching his sermon, he would have altar call prayer. As Rev. Smith was extending the invitation to come to the altar, I had my eyes closed. I suddenly felt the need to open my eyes. When I opened my eyes, I saw that my dad had been sitting on the back seat. He walked to the front of the church and fell on the altar. With tears streaming from his eyes and rolling down his cheek, he asked God for forgiveness of his sins and he gave his heart to Jesus. For the first time I saw father show emotions in a positive way. He cried and cried. He laid on the altar and eventually Rev Smith lifted his arm to help him stand to his feet. Rev. Smith looked in my father's eyes and he asked "are you ready to be saved? My father shouted "Yes, yes I want to be saved. Just like he did for me when I came to altar, he told my father to repeat after him. My father did and he accepted Jesus as his Lord and Savior. Right before my eyes God had answered my prayer.

After my father had accepted Jesus in his heart, Rev. Smith told me and my mom to come to the altar. That was the moment when everything in my life changed for the good. We walked in the church divided as a family but we left there united as one.

MY DADDY'S LOVE

Chapter 16

AFTER MY DAD ACCEPTED JESUS into his heart as his Lord and Savior, my dad was a new man. His attitude and his outlook on life changed. We didn't have to worry about the mood that he would be in when he came home from work. He came home on time and acted as if he was glad to see us. Instead of secluding himself and spending countless hours in his "man" cave, he would spend time in the family room with me and my mom watching television or playing board games. He didn't just send us to church anymore, but now he went along with us. In fact, he was usually dressed and ready to go before we were. He even was eager to hear about what Ms. Bertha was teaching.

Life at our home was different. It was different, but in a good way. For one, things were better between my mom and my dad. They were spending quality time together like they did when they were first married. They had even started having date night every Saturday night. Date night meant that only the two of them went out together. Sometimes they would have dinner at a nice restaurant and then go to the movie theater to see the latest movie feature. Then there were other times that they would take a moonlight stroll in the park. It didn't matter where they went, as long as they were together and could spend time alone without any interruptions from me or my brother. To make certain that that happened; they had a "no children allowed every on date night". I don't know how Charles felt about it, but I was okay with it. With all the things that my family had been through, I think that they deserved to have that time together.

It was a welcome sight to see my father and mother praying together, instead of arguing with one another about everything under the sun. My mom did most of the praying because my dad did not feel comfortable praying at least not out loud anyway. The reason that he didn't feel comfortable was because he thought that he didn't know the right words to say to God. My mom tried to explain to my dad that praying was simply having a conversation with God and that if he knew how to talk then he knew how to pray. Perhaps still feeling insecure, he still insisted that she continue to lead them in prayer during their prayer time that they had together. My mom did not mind at all. Actually that was one of her favorite things to do. My dad knew that too. There were many times that my dad would fuss because my mom was always off somewhere to herself praying to God. He would get upset with her because when situations would arise or they were facing some difficult challenge, her response would always be; let's pray about it. Those simple words would drive my daddy crazy. He didn't understand the power of prayer. But my mom was convinced that one day he would understand. But for now, she would continue to be the prayer leader as she and my dad kneeled down at the foot of their bed each night before they went to bed.

Another thing that brought joy to my heart was seeing my dad read the bible with my mom. My dad had never read the bible before. He did not even own a bible. He had heard a few things about the bible, but did not know much about the bible. In fact, there were some things that I knew that he didn't know. I knew more than he did because of what mama; Grandma Mattie and Ms. Bertha taught me.

One of the requirements of being accepted as a member of the church was to attend Christian discipline classes. Being a new member, my dad had started attending those classes. He learned how to increase his walk with God. He was learned more about God's love and the power of forgiveness. He learned about his role as a husband and his leadership role as head the household. Through studying the scriptures, he learned what his responsibility as a father is. Some of the key scriptures that he was taught was Ephesians 6:4, which says

"And ye fathers, provoke not your children to wrath, but bring them up in the nurture and the admonition of the Lord". He also learned that Proverbs 22:6 says "Train up a child in the way that he should go and when he is old, he will not depart from it". It was through those scriptures that my dad realized that he had not fulfilled his obligation as a father. It was through those classes that he was able to get in touch with reality and understand that his absence as a loving and supportive father had devastated my life. He finally understood that although he was physically present in my life, his emotional absence left a void in my life.

He had not provided a safe environment where there was love and acceptance. I had grown up knowing that my father did not love me, but not really understanding why. Every child needs to see their parents working together as a team and not divided against one another. He did not set a good example for me to follow, as every good parent should. He had not taught me the ways of the Lord. He certainly had not taken the time to help my mom raise me. It is sad to say, but people on the outside of our home had a provided more guidance to help keep me on the right path, than my father had.

Nevertheless he was making changes. Both my mom and I could see the changes that God was making in my dad's life. He was indeed a different man. I was becoming more to him than someone who merely existed, but I was someone who he wanted to be a part of his life. In my mind, my dad went from being my father to my daddy. Watching him make that transition from being a father to becoming my dad was awe inspiring. He finally understood how important his role as father was in my life. I was tempted to ask myself the question "is this a dream? If it was I sure didn't want to wake up.

Gradually my dad and I started spending time together. We did a lot of things together as a family, but my dad made it a point to make special time for the two of us. One of our favorite things to do was to go to the basketball games. Before now, he really didn't know that I liked basketball as much as I did. It was not as nearly as much as I liked writing, but I did like basketball. I could see the guilt in my dad's eyes when I told him that it was Uncle Jim who took me to my first college basketball game. My dad could not afford to take me to the game at the big stadium and to eat at a fancy restaurant after the game, like Uncle Jim had done for me. Instead we went to the local high school basketball games and we ate a fast food restaurant. That was all that my dad could afford and I was okay with that. It was different from going to the game with Uncle Jim than with my dad because it was not any interior motives with my dad. It was just an innocent game of basketball between a father and his daughter.

Although we were spending time together, there were still some hurdles that we had to overcome as a father and daughter team. For one thing we really did not know how to communicate effectively with one another. I did not know how to open up to my dad because we had never really had a heart to heart father daughter conversation. We had never bonded together. In the back of my mind, I was still thinking that things were the same as they always were; my dad criticizing me for everything that I did or said. I could not seem to wrap my mind around the fact that things were different now and it was now safe to freely express myself and tell my dad what was on my mind and tell him how I felt. I did not know how to be a part of my dad's life and he really didn't know how to be a part of mine. It sounds simple, but in so many ways it was one of the most difficult things to do. It was hard trying to figure out just how do I include my dad in my life, when he had been absent for so long.

It kind of reminded me of a television show that I saw. This woman's husband had suddenly vanished. He had been missing for fifteen years. Throughout this whole time, she did not hear from him. She did not know if he was dead or alive. Since he had not heard from him, her only assumption was that he was dead. She had learned to live her life alone. Then all of a sudden, just out of the clear blue sky, he appears on her front door step wanting to reenter her life with a simple I am sorry that I didn't contact you before now. That is how I felt. Here I was all of this time, pleading with my dad to take an active role in life. But he abandoned me emotionally. He was missing in my life. Then suddenly he gets a wakeup call and appears in my life and wants to take an active role. Just like that woman I had grown accustomed to living my life without him. My emotions were torn between being happy that God had answered my prayer and upset because it took so long for my dad to realize that I needed him.

We were working together, but I knew that it would take time and work to bridge the gap between my dad and me. It was much easier for my mom and dad to work on mending their relationship. That is because they already had a foundation to build on. They could draw from the love and trust that they had when they were first married and move forward. But it was not like that with me and my dad's relationship. We did not have much of a foundation. Every relationship, whether it is husband and wife or parent and child, should be built on love, acceptance, and trust. The relationship between me and my father did not have those qualities. Until now my dad has never displayed his love toward me nor did he accept me as his daughter therefore we didn't have anything to build from. We didn't have any special father and daughter memories in which we can reminisce about. Based on those facts alone it would seem that our relationship was hopeless. It would take some work, but I was convinced that with God's help we would build a strong father and daughter relationship. God had already taken our relationship from the point of me barely existing in my dad's eyes, to him making a conscious effort to be a part of my life. God had already brought us thus far and he was not going to leave us now.

Sure there were things that we had to work on, like learning how to build trust for one another and learning how to effectively communicate with one another, but we were on the road to recovery headed in the direction that I had longed for so long as a young child.

Just knowing that I had my daddy's acceptance and to hear my daddy say to me that he loves me, made every effort in trying to establish a healthy relationship worthwhile. Although our relationship was not perfect, with my daddy's love, I felt empowered. With his support, I felt as though I could accomplish any goal that I set my mind too.

THE CHANGE IN ME

Chapter 17

NOT ONLY DID MY DAD change, but I changed as well. In the beginning I was on a quest to win my daddy's love, but that quest turned into a journey that I had embarked on to find my self worth and the understanding of my significance in Christ. Yes, I was still just as eager to build a relationship with my father, but I had a greater desire to build a relationship with God. Deeper than the longing that I had for my dad's acceptance and approval, was my longing to grow closer and develop a relationship with God.

In many ways, I am grateful for my struggle in trying to gain my father's love. For it was through the struggle, that brought me closer to God. Although I endured some painful experiences as a result of the absence of my father's love, I still none the less learned some very valuable lessons. I am convinced that Mrs. Campbell was right when she said that you can't make a person love you. It takes God. Through all of my human efforts, I tried my best to show my dad that I was deserving of his love, but it was not until God intervened and with his infinite wisdom orchestrated a plan to bring me and my dad together. It was the through the implementation of God's plan that caused my dad to realize the importance and honor it was to be my father. God showed me that only real true love comes from him. I realized that I had mistakenly boxed God, my heavenly Father into the same category as my earthly father. God is not like my daddy because God is able to look past my imperfections and shortcomings and still love me whereas with my daddy it was because of my shortcomings and my imperfections that drove him away from me. Through his unconditionally love, God always accepts us just the way we are.

Another lesson that I learned was that that God is a forgiving God. Out of the all the things that had happened to me in life, I realized that I had a choice to be better or to be bitter. I could continue living life full of unforgiveness in my heart internalizing bitterness and hatred and stay trapped in a chaotic mindset or I could exercise my right to forgive and be forgiven and release myself from turmoil and live in peace and harmony as God had designed. I chose to be better.

Another lesson that I learned was that it does not matter what happens in your life, and no matter how broken you are, God is able to heal every scar. I was emotionally scared of course from the verbal and physical abuse from my dad and the ultimate betrayal by my Uncle Jim. Grandma Mattie's death had left an empty black hole in my heart that out of desperation, I tried to fill it with the wrong things. But through all of that, God showed me that even when I am at my lowest point in life, he is able to pick me up and put in a position to receive healing. That is exactly what he had done. He had begun the healing process and was extracting all of the pain that my scars and wounds had caused and he began to transform me to a new person.

He transformed my life from being a broken, bitter and insecure little girl to a mature, complete and emotional stable young woman. He peeled back all the layers of insecurity that the physical, emotional and sexually abuse had caused in my life, one layer at a time. As he peeled back those layers, I found out more about myself and who I was and who I was to become. One thing for sure, I was not the little girl who was once in hot pursuit of her daddy's love because I had found that true love in my relationship with God.

Reflecting back on some of the lessons that I had learned from Ms. Bertha and Rev. Smith's sermons, was what challenged me to want to develop a deeper relationship with God. They had both emphasized the importance of getting to know God for myself. They would both say "I can tell you all day long how good God is and what he will do for you in your life, but it is nothing like experiencing him for yourself." God himself had demonstrated to me his ability to transform a person's life, through the evidence of a transformation of my own life and of my dad's life. He had proven to me that I was significant enough to him for him to answer my prayers. He had indeed answered my prayer about saving my daddy and bringing our family back together.

The more I read and studied the scriptures in the bible, the more I learned about God. The more I learned about him, the thirstier I became and the more I wanted to learn about Him. The hungrier and thirstier I became, the stronger my faith in God became and my desire to see his awesome power of God move in my life became that more powerful. Being in a relationship with God gave me the encouragement that I needed to stretch my faith and to believe that within me lied the power to overcome any obstacle that came in my way. With this newfound love that I had found Christ, I learned to believe in myself. I had a passion to pursue all of my God given dreams. The dreams that I had once put on the back shelf of my mind because someone in the past had said that it could not be done or that I didn't have what it took to make it happen, were the dreams that I had the courage to pursue. But I had read the word of God and in it I found one key verse that I lived by. It is found in the Philippians 4:13 "I can do all things through Christ which strengthen me". To me God was telling me that I could do anything that I set my mind too because I had Christ's strength.

There were many other scriptures that I read that encouraged me, but that one verse kept the fire flaming in my heart. It was the verse that I referred too if I was ever in doubt about my ability to achieve any goal that I had set. It was the verse that I stood on when I made the decision to pursue my dream to become a published author. With much determination, I stepped out on faith and entered my first writing contest. In that contest the stakes were high. The grand prize was $100,000 and the winner would also receive a publishing contract with one of the participating publishing companies. I had decided that I would compile all of my journal entries that I had written in the past about how I felt living life without my father's love. I guess I could have chosen to write about anything, but I wanted to write about something that was near and dear to my heart.

I wanted to write about something that I had experienced myself first hand. I knew about the pain of others classifying you as a statistic and having low expectations of your success based on the fact that I did not have parental involvement from my dad. I could identify with the misery of being rejected because I was not wanted by my dad, and the embarrassment of having a father living in the same home with you physically, but emotionally drawn from you.

I poured blood, sweat, and tears into making this the best book that I could. I had several of my friends and teachers to read it to make sure that I had made sure that I did not make any mistakes. Then once I felt that it sounded good enough and that everything flowed together, I prayed about it and then I submitted it into the contest. I was proud of myself because I had the courage to pursue my dream. You might be wondering if I worked for Mr. Frank Simmons and had saved enough money why didn't I just use that money. That is a good question. I had prayed to God about pursuing my dream of becoming a published author, and his clear instructions were to enter contests. He did not tell me to buy a publishing package from a company, he simply told me to enter various contests. One thing that I had learned was that it was always best to follow God's instructions. So that is what I did.

I waited patiently for the deadline for entering the contest. After the contest was closed and there would not be any more entries accepted, I had to wait another three weeks to find out if my manuscript had been selected as a winner. To keep myself encouraged, I kept reading God's word and confessing that I was going to be one of the winners. I would even envision myself walking across the stage and hearing my name called as one of the winners. The three week time frame had passed and it was now time to find out the results of the contest. Everyone who had entered the contest was both nervous and excited. Mrs. Davis was too.

Mr. Becktrim came on the PA system just as he always did to make the morning announcements. To be honest, usually I don't really listen to all the announcements that he makes, only to the ones that I think apply to me. This morning was different because this morning he had my full attention. I did not want to miss anything that he said, just in case he said something about the contest winners.

I listened attentively; he did not mention a single thing about the contest. Then at the end of the announcements, he asked Mrs. Davis to come to the office. Mrs. Davis looked surprised about her summons to the office just as I did. I couldn't help but wonder if her being called to the office had something to do with the contest. Mrs. Davis went across the hall to the next class to ask if Mrs. Troutman, the paraprofessional in Mrs. Galor's class could possibly watch her class until she returned from the office. Mrs. Galor came and sat in our classroom until Mrs. Davis returned.

Mrs. Davis returned with a stack of papers in her hand. As she ciphered through the papers, she had a dull look on her face indicating that what she was reading was not of much interest to her. But then she came across a shiny semi gloss gold envelope, and a big smile came shining across her face. I assumed that what she was holding in her hand were the results of the contest. My assumption was correct. The results were sent to school addressed to Mrs. Davis.

With much excitement and anticipation, she ripped opened the envelope. She read the letter silently at first and she shared the good news with the class. She said "I am pleased to announce that Rebecca, Stephanie, and Michelle and Stacey Alexander, you all have been selected as one of the winners of the ABC writing contest. You all will be attending the awards ceremony this year. Mrs. Davis told us that the letter did not specify who had won first place, second place or third place or who the grand prize winner was. Of course everyone wants to win the grand prize, but I was perfectly satisfied with just knowing that I had been selected as one of the winners.

I could not wait to get home to tell both my mom and my dad. I ran screeching down the hallway short of breath trying to spit my words out to my mom that I had won the contest. She told me to calm down and talk slow so she could understand. Inhaling and then exhaling, I told my mom that I had won the contest; well at least I had placed in the contest. As always she was just as excited as I was about me winning. She was always happy for me when something good happened to me. I told her about the awards ceremony. She immediately went to fashion designer mode, and started telling me the color and the type of dress that I should wear and what kind of accessories that I should wear. The thing about my mom was that I had not even told her that I had the possibility of winning $100,000 if I was selected as the grand prize winner. She did not know anything about any of the prizes and she was still happy for me. That showed me that she was genuine when she said that she was proud of me.

It was almost time for my dad to get home from work. I sat outside on the swing in our front yard. I wanted to make sure that I got first dibs on him before my mom got to him. In all of her excitement, sometimes my mom would get carried away and tell all of the good news before the other person gets to tell it for themselves. I wanted to make sure that I was the one who told my daddy first.

As he drove up in the car, and as soon as he put the gear in park, I snatched opened the door. He looked rather surprised and wondered what warranted an inviting welcome home of this kind. I looked at him and told him that I had been selected as one of the winners in the writing contest that our school was hosting. I told him that I did not know if I had won first, second or third place, or even if I was the overall winner. He gave me a big hug and said that it didn't matter what position I won, first, second or third, that he was proud of me. Wow! Words cannot explain how that made me feel. Those words "I am proud of you" sent chills down my spine.

I told my dad about the awards ceremony. With a big beam of light in his eye, he said "see I told you that one day you were going to dress up and I was going to escort you to a special event". We both looked at each other and smiled.

My mom and I went shopping for my dress to wear to the ceremony. We found a beautiful orange sequin dress with rhinestones. I had clear shoes with a hint of orange in the rhinestones Ms. Mary did my hair just the way I wanted it for the Father Daughter dance.

When we arrived at the ceremony, we were greeted by the friendly staff. They told us where we were to be seated and that a table had been reserved for each of the selected winners. My family and I were assigned to the very last table. Was this any indication that my book had been selected in third place?

The ceremony started and the announcer welcomed everyone and he gave special recognition to all of the winners. He gave us in house information such as where the restrooms were, and he asked everyone to please turn off their cell phones or at least put them on vibrate. He then began to call the names of the winners. 1st place, Ms. Rebecca Walker, 2nd place, Ms. Stephanie Green, 3rd place, Ms, Michelle Burrows. Everyone was standing and giving each of the girls a standing ovation. But what a minute, what is going on? Why didn't he call my name?

The announcer asked that everyone get quiet and take their seats. Then with a drum roll, he announced "our grand prize winner is Ms. Stacey Alexander. Can you imagine how I felt? I was the youngest author that this company had ever published a book for. Just like before the whole audience was applauding and giving me a standing ovation. It was a dream come true. Winning the money was great, but knowing that I had pursued and achieved my dream was a much gratifying reward.

My dad was right in that this day meant more to me than the Father Daughter dance ever could. As my dad escorted me across the stage to receive my award, he leaned over to me and said "You are a great writer Stacey, I am so proud of you and I love you.

Everyone in my family and my community made a big deal about me being the grand prize winner of the contest. My aunts and uncles planned a surprise party for me to celebrate. It was a nice gesture and I really did appreciate it, but it kind of made me sad a little because I wished Grandma Mattie could have been there with us. It was times like those that I missed her the most. It felt awkward celebrating with her, especially since she was one of the main people in my life who had encouraged me to pursue my dream of becoming a writer. Nevertheless I pulled myself together and embraced the festivities that my family had worked so hard to plan. After all that is the way that Grandma Mattie would have wanted it.

The taste of success sent my self esteem soaring beyond what I could have ever imagined. Winning the writing contest was the catalyst for other great things to happen in my life. It gave me the determination to set goals for myself and the ammunition to achieve them.

One of the goals that I wanted to achieve was to make honor roll in school. It might sound simple, and not weigh heavy of the scale of efficient goal setting, but it was something that I wanted to do. I wanted to prove not only to myself that I could do it, but I also wanted to show my dad that with his support I could do it. I also wanted Mrs. Campbell to know that I had what it took to be successful. She had written me off in her mind and was determined that I would never be successful. Based on her years of teaching experience and working with hundreds of students, she was able to distinguish between which of her students would make successful productive citizens and the ones who would only work at a merger wage paying jobs. She had classified me with those students in the latter group. One thing that I did not like was too but given a label. I was determined more than ever to prove Mrs. Campbell wrong. I made up my mind that I was not going to sit idly by and just accept her view of who I was and what I could or could not accomplish. One thing that I did not understand was that if Mrs. Campbell grew up without her father being in her life, and some how she had beat the odds and surpassed the statistical view of what society suggested that she would become, then why didn't she think that I could achieve the same goal.

Regardless of what she or anyone else thought I was determined that I would become a better student and I would achieve my goal of being on the honor roll. I knew that in order to move in the right direction of being an honor roll student, I had to change my study habits. Instead of waiting before I started preparing for a test, as soon as my teachers would give me the information that would be covered on the test, I began to study that night. I did not procrastinate. When it came to getting my projects completed, I made sure that I allowed myself enough time to gather the necessary research so I would not feel pressured at the last minute. Every day I started on my homework as soon as I came home. That way I would not be too tired and sleepy to finish it later that night.

Although I felt uncomfortable and did not like asking for help from my teachers, I started raising my hand and asking questions in class when I did not have a clear understanding about something.

As Mrs. Campbell had vicariously pointed out to my mom, I had always struggled in school. From the time that I entered kindergarten to now, I always had some type of difficulty in school. There were a few subjects that I liked and did really well in, such as Language Arts. Although reading comprehension was a challenge for me, reading was one of my favorite subjects as well. I liked to read. I was intrigued with turning the pages of our crisp new novels and reading about the adventurous characters who engaged in dangerous plots and schemes. The one and only time in school that I didn't mind the teacher calling on me was when I was in my language arts class. In elementary school, I absolutely loved it when the teacher would write sentences on the board and she would call us to go to the board to underline the specified part of speech in the sentence. I guess looking back now that seems a bit childish, but the fun part about it was that if we got the answer right we would get a prize usually a piece of candy.

Another thing that made learning in my language arts class exciting was being in competition with the teacher. I liked it when the teacher would always issue a challenge to the students. It was the students against the teacher. That made me want to do my best so that we could win. After all what student would not want to have the bragging rights to say that they had defeated their teacher. Although I liked writing just slightly better than reading, I learned how to become a better writer in my Language arts class.

I knew that I had to work hard in all of my classes, not just the classes that I liked. I couldn't just focus on language arts or reading, but I had to dedicate equal time to the subjects that I was not good at. Science and Social Studies were my biggest challenges. There were some things about science that I liked, but I most assuredly detested Social Studies. I can't really pinpoint one thing in particular that I didn't like about it, I just knew that overall Social Studies was my least favorite subject.

It didn't matter whether I liked the subject or not, I had to work hard if I wanted to achieve my goal. I would have to work hard throughout the entire duration of the semester. In the past I would usually start off strong studying, and completing all of my assignments and handing them in on time. But for some reason the last couple of weeks or so in the semester, I would start to lose my motivation and my grades suffer as a result of that.

This time I believed that things would be different. This time I was determined that I would do whatever I had to do to make honor roll. There times that I had to burn some midnight oil in order for me to get my assignments completed for the next day. But I had no doubt that it would be worth it.

MY FIRST HONOR ROLL

Chapter 18

THE END OF THE SEMESTER had come upon us and it was time for the teachers to tally our grades so that we could see the final outcome. As always we had to wait in suspense until the end of the day before we got our report cards. I guess Mr. Becktrim wanted the teachers to wait until the end of the day to prevent the raucous of the students spending precious time comparing grades instead of paying attention to the teacher.

As did the other students, I wanted anxiously to the end of the day. The school bell rung early to dismiss us from 6th period so we could go back to our homeroom class. Since my mom had me removed out of Mrs. Campbell's class, Mrs. Davis was now my academic teacher and my homeroom teacher. We don't go to our homeroom every day, just when the school needs to get some important information to us for us to take home to our parents. Today we had to go back to homeroom to get what I considered the most important information, our report card.

Quickly glancing over each student's record card, Mrs. Davis called each student to her desk to come and receive their report card. She called Carl, with a smile she handed him his report card. She continued to call the names of each student and each time she had a different expression on her face. It was an expression none the less that signified that she was pleased with what she saw. She finally called my name. She looked me in my eye, with no kind of expression on her face just a deep penetrating blank stare. She had simply picked the other students report cards off her desk and handed it to them, but she took the time and folded my paper in half and then handed mine to me.

With my confidence down by a notch, I reached out to grab my report card. Mrs. Davis placed my report card in my hand and she smiled and said "Congratulations! Job well done! I looked at my paper with excitement. I strolled down each column to see the teacher's name, subject and the grade that I had received in each class. I looked at all of my grades, I had made 5 A's 1 B. In the right corner at the bottom of my report card, I saw the prettiest gold star affixed next to the message Final average" 96. Congratulations! Honor Roll Student!!

I did it! I reached my goal. All of my hard work was not in vain and it had paid off! I was super excited about making honor roll. As always whenever something good happened at school, I would be excited about going home to tell my mom and dad. That is exactly what I did. I went home and parading around just like a little kid who just ate a box of candy, showing my mom and dad my report card.

They both expressed that they were proud of me, but of course as always my mom showed her emotions more openly than my dad did. My mom was jumping up and down with me. We were both like a little kid who was a sugar rush from eating so much candy. Excitement filled the air. This time my mom did not have to worry about finding a frame to put my certificate in, I had already beaten her to it. I had found an old picture frame lying around. Well actually the picture frame wasn't just lying around, I took a picture of an old guy sitting at a fish creek with his fishing pole out of the picture frame and I used it to be my report card in it.

It is beyond my imagination, why I did not just ask my mom to buy a new picture frame. I am more than sure that she would have especially for an occasion such as this. But I didn't ask her too. I guess I did not want to wait long enough for her to go to the store. I wanted instant gratification of being able to hang my report card on the wall so that I could look at it as much as I wanted too.

This was the first time that I had ever made honor roll since I had started school, but it was not the last time. From that point on, I continued to study hard and each semester I made honor roll. I maintained an "A" average the remainder time that I was in high school. Each time that my mom would see my grades, she would say to me "see I knew that you had it in you, you just had to bring it out".

Because my grades had improved and I had consecutively made honor roll, I was invited to be a part of the National Beta Club. The Beta Club was an organization that recognized young people.

Just like my middle school years, time had flown by and now my high school days were coming to an end. Just like my transition from middle to high school was bitter sweet, I find myself in the same state of mind now. The beginning of high school I was faced with the challenge of adapting to a new surrounding and overcoming the obstacles in Mrs. Campbell's class. Now I was faced with the challenge of adjusting to life after high school. I was entering the world of adulthood. I would have an opportunity to put all of the training that I had received in high school in action and become a productive citizen in society. This was exciting as well as fearful.

The exciting part was actually graduating from school. The fact that being out school meant that I did not have to get up early in the morning to get ready for school. I did not have to choose between spending time with my friends and spending time studying. There were no more nights staying up late working on homework assignments. For those reasons I was glad to reach this milestone in my life.

During my senior year I was chosen as the most improved student. I went from being a struggling low self-esteem student to a high achieving student who had a bright future. I had made so much of a significant change in my both my academics, my personal life, and my outlook on life, that I was chosen to be the student speaker at our graduation ceremony. Imagine me the same girl who could barely stand in front of Mrs. Campbell's class and read a simple journal entry about my father, now I will have the opportunity to stand before hundreds and speak. Talk about something being ironic.

That goes to show just how much I had grown in walk with Christ. It was because of my relationship with Jesus that I had the courage to begin this journey to living a life free of insecurities. God had replaced those ill feelings that I had about myself with a strong belief that I am valuable and that with him I could accomplish any goal that I set my mind too. I could overcome every obstacle that came in my way. I knew that apart from God that I could not make it. I would not have ever won the contest, I would not be graduating at the top of my class and I certainly would not have been chosen to the student speaker. This was all because of God and I gave him all the credit.

Besides self-gratification, knowing that I was making my daddy proud of me was one of the reasons that I worked to achieve my dreams. His love and support was what fueled the engine of my life. The very thought that of having my dad's support kept my heart pumping and eager to dig deeper, set the next goal and achieve it. Growing up as a young child, all I ever wanted was to know that my daddy loved me, and that he was proud of me. I had reached the point where I had conquered that mission.

My dad loved me and he was proud. I could tell before then, but I could especially tell when he saw me on my graduation day. I could only imagine what was going through his mind on that day. A day that he thought would never happen. Sadly, my dad's perception of my future was limited to the fact in his mind that I would never earn my diploma, but I would only receive a certificate stating that I had attended school for twelve years. Thank God, he was wrong. This reminds me of what my Grandma Mattie used to say. She said that it doesn't matter what a person thinks about you or what they say about you, everybody is entitled to their opinion, but it doesn't necessary make it right. She also taught me that people would try to put a label on you and try to limit your abilities based what they think, but you don't have to accept what they say. Now I had a clear meaning of what she was talking about. My dad, Mrs. Campbell and many others had labeled me, but I fought against what they were saying and defeated the odds.

As I, along with the rest of the graduates, marched in the auditorium, I could see a host of family members and friends with smiles on their faces and some with tissues in their hands. They were just as eager as we were to celebrate this momentous occasion; and rightly so. They had each played their significant role in helping each graduate get to that point in life.

The ceremony began promptly at 2:00. Mr. Becktrim approached the podium to address the audience "Before we begin this joyous ceremony, let me remind you to turn off your cell phones and be courteous to those around you by refraining from talking during the ceremony. We encourage you to express your pride by applauding and cheering, but the use of air horns is expressly forbidden. Please enjoy the ceremony. With his best effort, he tried to express the severity of what the consequences would be for those who choose not to adhere to the guidelines of showing respect to each of the graduates. He said it in a diplomatic way, but in simple layman terms he was basically saying was if any one acted uncivilized, that the police would gladly escort them out of the auditorium. I knew that that was a rule that was sure to be broken. There is always someone in the crowd who will have a bullhorn or some other type of noisemaker to stir up the crowd. To be honest, I really don't blame them. It seems to me that they would want the family to celebrate with the graduates. That is as long as if they showed respect to all of the graduates.

With the assurance that everyone present fully understood the rules, Mr. Becktrim proceeded with the ceremony. He said "Welcome to our Spring Graduation Ceremony. We will now begin. Please join me in honoring our graduates and welcoming faculty and staff". The audience stood and gave a sounding applause.

Following Mr. Bectrim's address was Dr. Ruth Wetherinspoon's, our school superintendent, welcome address. Dr. Wetherinspoon had a very loud and boisterous personality. At every function that she attended she was sure to capture the attention of the audience to whom she was speaking. One thing that everyone knew about Dr. Wetherinspoon was that she had a passion for young people. She welcomed an opportunity given to her to pour into the lives of young people. I was certain that this occasion would serve as a catalyst for her to build upon her platform to encourage students to stay in school and graduate.

Dr. Wetherinspoon was allotted 15 minutes to address the audience, but of course as always she exceeded her time. It was perfectly okay with me because according to the program I was the next speaker. The longer that she talked, the longer I had to stay in my seat and get my nerves together.

To say that I was nervous was an understatement. But why? I mean I had actually practiced saying my speech in front of the mirror several times. I had even let my mom listen to me say my speech. I was still nervous. I could feel my knees knocking together like they were playing their own symphony. My hands were sweaty and my heart was skipping a beat. There were thumping and pounding sensations going through my head so forceful that I wondered if the veins in my head would pop out. It was the same feeling that I had when I was in Mrs. Campbell's class. I was reliving the torture all over again.

Just like I had done when I was in Mrs. Campbell's class, I contemplated ways of how I could get out of the situation. Maybe I could say that I was sick and then I wouldn't have to deal with speaking in the front of all those people.

I sat there with my mind racing back and forth. If I just had some way of knowing that everything would be okay, then my mind could be at ease. But all I could seem to imagine was me getting out of my seat and trip and fall. Or if I actually make it to the podium, I will have another case of my mouth not cooperating with my brain. I just need reassurance that everything would be alright. I realized that the only way that I had of knowing that things would work out was to pray to God; so I did. Mumbling under my breath, I said a simple prayer. "Lord, I know that you have not given me the spirit of fear, but of power and of love and of a sound mind, but I am afraid. Will you give me peace in my spirit and let me know that everything is going to be alright"? Just then I glanced across the audience, and I saw my dad hold his two thumbs up along with the biggest smile I have ever seen on his face. Then all of sudden a calm and warm feeling came over me and I knew then that everything would be alright.

Just shortly after this encounter that I had with God, Dr. Wetherinspoon ended her speech. Mr. Becktrim approached the podium and made the announcement that twenty minutes ago I was dreading. He said "It is now my pleasure to invite to the podium, Ms. Stacey Alexander, our student speaker. Graduates welcome your classmate, Stacey Alexander"

I rose from my seat and walked to the podium. All was well so far. I opened my mouth and began to speak. I spoke eloquently and proficiently, without any trouble at all. It was as if God was given me an opportunity to shine; not to inflate my ego, but to show the world what he had known about me along, and that was I had the potential for greatness. I took this advantageous opportunity to encourage and empower my fellow classmates about some of the valuable lessons that I had learned on this journey called life. I shared my insight about this powerful force called love. I wanted it to be clear that they each understood that love was powerful in the sense that it had the ability to act as an agent for transformation or obliteration in a person's life. I had had a taste of both worlds. Knowing the impact that having both my heavenly Father's love and my earthly father's love had on my life; I issued a challenge to each of the graduates. My challenge was for each graduate to do soul searching and become channels of extending love to someone who is in dire need of feeling acceptance, love and support.

After I finished with my speech, the entire audience once again stood and gave me a standing ovation. There was whistle blowing and I even heard someone blow a bull horn. I couldn't help but feel joy in my heart not because I made through the speech, but because I was graduating from high school and my dad was there to witness it. To have my dad's presence was a demonstration of God's love for me. It was because of God's love that my dad's heart was changed.

Now it was time for what we had all been waiting for. It was time to receive our diplomas in our hands once and for all. It is so amazing how we spend countless hours studying for tests, working diligently to complete our projects, staying up late to make sure all our homework is done, all in the name of a piece of paper with our names written on it. Well, maybe it was more to it than that, but you will have to admit that it would be nice if the school would at least offer a reward of some kind to those who have completed twelve years of school. What if the school would provide every graduate with a new car of their choice? That would be absolutely amazing, but I doubt that would ever happen.

With our diplomas in his hand, Mr. Becktrim said "It is now my honor to certify the candidates for their diplomas. Dr. Wetherinspoon on behalf of the faculty, I certify to you that those candidates who have completed all of their academic requirements are entitled to receive their respective diplomas. Both Mr. Becktrim and Dr. Wetherinspoon stood as our names were called out and we walked across the stage to receive our diplomas.

They called my friend, David Allen. Everyone clapped. I was next in line. My name was called. My dad stood and clapped his hands, screaming that's my baby girl. My baby is graduating.

Trying her best to silence my dad, my mom leaned over to my dad and said "See I told you that with a little encouragement she would make it"

Now that graduation was over, we were each faced with the decision of exploring options for the next phase of life. I had already applied to several colleges that I thought that I might be interested in. Some of the colleges that I had submitted application for enrollment were in our local area and some were a few hundred miles away from home. Neither my mom nor my dad wanted me to move away. To be quite honest, although I had entertained the idea of living on my own, I really wasn't ready to move out just yet.

Every day I checked the mailbox for acceptance letters from colleges. I did receive some letters back from various colleges, but unfortunately that were the colleges that were far away. I will admit it felt good to know that because of my grades, I could actually choose what school I wanted to attend. Before I was inspired to work hard at being successful in school, I would not have had this opportunity to choose. My choices would have been limited. But now I had options and it made me feel proud of myself.

But although I could have chosen any one of the schools that had sent me an acceptance letter, I did not feel led to go. Many of friends had already made up their minds that they were going to move as far away as they could as quick as they could. They were ready to experience the good life or at least what they thought was the good life. They tried to convince me to move along with them, but I knew that was totally out of the question for me. I didn't have any desire to experience what they considered the good life.

Even if I wanted to leave, I couldn't. There was something that was compelling me to stay in my community. I thought maybe God had more work to do with me and my dad's relationship. We had come a long way when it came to our relationship, but in many ways it didn't feel as though the mission was complete. Maybe he had a special assignment.

Against the advice of my friends, I stayed in our hometown and went to the local college. I had decided that I wanted to become a teacher. Of course I wanted to be a language arts teacher since that was my favorite subject throughout the entire time I was in school. I was fortunate enough that every language arts teacher that I had was a good teacher, but Mrs. Davis was the one who really inspired me to become a teacher. She had the ability to reach every student regardless of what level he or she was on. She created a thirst for knowledge. She made me want to learn. That was the main reason that I wanted to become a teacher, but another reason was because I didn't want any student to every have to go through what I went through in Mrs. Campbell's class. No, I will not be able to save every student, but at least I can do my part and help the ones that I can. I wanted to be that shining light and that ray of hope in a child's life, just like Mrs. Davis was for me. She believed in me when I didn't believe in myself.

Not only did I have a desire to teach academics, but I also had a passion to teach God's word. It was because of the lessons that Ms. Bertha, my grandma Mattie and the life that my mom lived before me that I had become the person that I was. My life had been impacted through the Word of God and I wanted the privilege of impacting other lives as well.

It was not long before Rev. Smith asked if I would be willing to teach the bible study classes for the elementary level. I told him that I would be more than honored. I begin to teach lessons to the girls just like Ms. Bertha had done for me. The girls that were in my class were from all walks of life. Some of the girls were from two parents home and were both emotionally and financially stable. There were some girls who were from single parent whose parents were struggling just to make ends meet. While I had a passion and a calling to work with all the girls, my heart went out to the few girls whose father was present in their lives physically, but emotionally they were absent. They were being taken care financially, but emotionally they were bankrupt. Those were the girls who pulled at my heart strings, because these were the girls that I could most identify with. The ones, who had both parents love and support, had what they needed. The girls, whose parents were struggling to take care of their financial wellbeing, could apply for assistance. If they were hungry, they could go to the soup kitchen. If they were in need of clothes, there were several churches that gave away free clothes. But where do you go when you are in the need of your father's love? I knew the pain of not having my father's love and the devastating affect that it had on my life. I did not want any of those girls to follow the same path that I had taken. I had made some bad choices in my life that undoubtedly I would not have made had I had my father's love and support. I had tried to kill myself because I was carrying so much pain in my heart. I did not want that for the girls in my class or for any girl as far as that goes. I wanted them to be equipped to handle any situation. I was blessed that my father eventually came around and God began to mend our relationship. But it was only after God had intervened in my dad's life that he realized his importance as a father. I knew that the fathers of those little girls needed to be enlighten on their important role as a father.

After much prayer, my father and I decided to join forces and to start our own organization called Daddy's Little Girl. It was a Christian based program that was dedicated to giving fathers the tools that they needed to be successful in fatherhood. Our organization provided guidance to both the daughters and their fathers on how to build a healthy bond in their relationship. Through various monthly activities and workshops, the men that participated were equipped to address the needs of their children and to understand the unique influence that they had on the life of their daughters. We wanted to ensure that children would have a brighter future by educating and engaging fathers. Based on the knowledge that a father's absence is strongly linked to poverty, teen pregnancy, juvenile delinquency, abuse and suicide, we stressed the importance of fathers taking an active role in the lives of their daughters.

As a result of working throughout the process with the other dads and their daughters, my dad and I grew stronger and closer together. We were learning how to effectively communicate with each other. We learned how to show each other love in a deeper way.

One of the most rewarding aspects of our program that I personally enjoyed was the group sessions that we held every Wednesday. This was a time set aside so that both the daughters and their fathers could share with each other or with the group as a whole. It was during that time they could tell about what was working in their relationship and what still needed work. It always did my heart good to hear success stories about how the gap had been bridged together between a father and his daughter.

In the beginning we had less than fifty men who actively participated in our program, but that number quickly grew well into the hundred's in just a short time. My dad played a very influential role in the growth of our membership, because he would reach out to others and invite them to come. It did not matter from what walk of life they had come, he made it known that they were welcomed. Many of the men would admit that they were a little apprehensive about sharing and acknowledging that they really did not know how to be a good father. Some of them had not had a good male role model in their lives. Some had been faced with having a father present in their life, but he had not set a good example for him to follow. While others, grew up with their father being absent.

My dad was chalked full of information and did not mind sharing what he had learned from about his role as a husband and a father. He was very instrumental in healing process of the other men who were a part of the group. It was through testimony that many of the men invited Christ in their lives and as a result became better fathers. He never failed to share with the group of men how God had intervened in his life and changed his heart. He changed his outlook on life and most importantly he changed how he felt about me.

My dad was very transparent when it came to him sharing the mistakes that he had made as a father. I would always shed a tear when I would hear him say that he had failed at being my father. He had missed out on the best part of my life because of his selfish ways. He shared that when I needed him the most, he was the farthest away. My dad regretted that so much time had lapsed before he decided to step up to the plate and assume his rightful position as a husband and a father.

He had regrets, but he also had some things that he was proud of. For one thing, he was glad that God had given him an opportunity to be get things right between me and him before it was too late. But he was also proud of the fact that I never gave up on him and the hope of establishing a loving father and daughter relationship. He laughs about it now, but he admits that during the times that I was telling him about Jesus and his love, that he didn't want to hear it. In fact that was the very last thing that he wanted to hear. But I was persistent, and kept telling him. He attributes my persistence to share God's word with him, and the demonstration of God's love that I had displayed by giving him one of my kidneys, was what really drew him to Christ.

Because of the impact that Daddy Little Girls organization has had on the lives of daughters and their fathers, we are often sought after to speak at various functions. When we are asked what our motivation for what we do is, we always look each other in the eye and say "this thing called love".